# THE HARDER I LAUGH,
# THE DEEPER I HURT

# THE HARDER I LAUGH, THE DEEPER I HURT

An Honest Look at Surviving Life's Pain

STAN TOLER +
DEBRA WHITE SMITH

BEACON HILL PRESS
OF KANSAS CITY

Copyright 2001, 2008
by Stan Toler and Debra White Smith

ISBN 978-0-8341-2377-9

Printed in the
United States of America

Cover Design: Arthur Cherry
Interior Design: Sharon Page

#### Library of Congress Cataloging-in-Publication Data

Toler, Stan.
    The harder I laugh the deeper I hurt : an honest look at surviving life's pain / Stan Toler and Debra White Smith.
        p. cm.
    Includes bibliographical references
    ISBN 978-0-8341-2377-9 (pbk.)
        1. Pain—Religious aspects—Christianity. 2. Laughter—Religious aspects—Christianity. 3. Christian life. I. Smith, Debra White. II. Title.

BV4909 .T65  2008
248.8'6—dc22

                                                                2008021547

10   9   8   7   6   5   4   3   2   1

In memory of my Grandma Brewster.
She suffered great pain and loss in life—
and all the while kept laughing!
—Stan Toler

For my friend Frances Shaw.
Also for my father, Gaylon L. White,
who taught me to always be a little wacky
and laugh, laugh, laugh!
—Debra White Smith

# CONTENTS

Weeping may remain

for a night,

but rejoicing comes

in the morning.

—Ps. 30:5

# FOREWORD

Stan and Debra have done quite a job in this book making me laugh. When I read Stan's account of being trapped in a Volkswagen, I cracked up. When I read Debra's story of her football-player-sized husband and the baby oil in the bathtub, I lost it. Or how about the story of the sink that broke loose and—oops! I don't want to give it all away!

I love to laugh, and I love to make people laugh. In fact, that's my job as a comedian. But even if it weren't my job, I would probably still tell a joke or two just to hear the laughs. Maybe not all of us can sing or speak in front of an audience, but we can all laugh. Indeed, we *must* laugh—that's what Stan and Debra firmly believe, for laughter is a sign of unbridled hope. And for moments when we may feel hopeless—during those times of heavy grief due to death, rejection, failure, or loss—then that beacon of hope is not only bright but warm and reassuring as well.

Though Stan and Debra write about things that will make you laugh, they also freely share their individual experiences with suffering, disappointment, and heartache. They tell how they were able to find the vibrant hope that's always just on the other side of the darkness. And it's there for you too. All you have to do is follow the sounds of the sweet, refreshing "Ha, ha, ha . . ."

—Chonda Pierce

# PREFACE

This book was inspired by secret pain in the lives of Christian people everywhere. Often we show up at church with a plastic smile, a few laughs, and an "I'm fine, thank you" when we're dying inside because of loss, depression, fear, or loneliness. Our sorrow is only increased by the well-meant but mistaken advice that "Christians don't get depressed" or "If you were really a Christian, you wouldn't struggle with negative emotions."

In fact, Christians do get depressed, and Christians do struggle with life's pain. We, Stan Toler and Debra White Smith, have experienced that reality firsthand. When I (Stan) was 11, my coal miner father, hoping to make a better life, moved our family from West Virginia to Columbus, Ohio. Being devout believers didn't spare the Toler family from tragedy, as my father was killed in a construction accident shortly after the move. I watched as my mother spiraled into depression. Our family loved the Lord and served Him completely. Yet tragedy struck, and I learned the unyielding nature of pain at a tender age.

When I (Debra) was 15, my family fell apart. During that lonely and confused time, I became the victim of sexual abuse. Like the Tolers, the White family loved the Lord. But our Christian faith did not prevent the tragic destruction of our family. We bear painful witness to the fact that Christians do suffer.

Both of us have overcome these devastating losses in our lives, in part by enjoying one of God's greatest gifts, laughter. The ability to find humor even in the most difficult circumstances has been an important element in our healing. Laughter has been the therapy that eased the pain and enabled us, along with our separate families, to carry on.

We're not alone. While we were working on this book, Oklahoma City was assaulted by a deadly tornado that left the city designated a national disaster area. We drove through the streets viewing the devastation and reviewing stories of homes destroyed and dreams annihilated. Through tears of sympathy, we noticed some words spray-painted on a half-destroyed home: "For sale, cheap: a real fixer-upper." Around the corner was another home with a sign that read, "House for sale: needs some work." Some survivors had chosen to put their sense of humor where their roofs used to be. They found laughter as a relief for pain.

You, too, have probably had your share of grief in life. As the Scripture rightly says, "Man is born to trouble as surely as sparks fly upward" (Job 5:7). Yet through it all, God can give a sense of joy. Laughter is a healing balm that covers our wounds and helps us discover the gracious, joy-filled God who reigns over all, including our sorrows and setbacks.

We hope that in the following pages you will discover both spiritual comfort and humorous relief for some of the pain in your life. Our purpose is not to answer the unanswerable "whys" of your life. Rather, our aim is to let you know that you're not alone.

You are not the first to hide your hurt with laughter. All of us have buried incidents in our lives that caused great pain. But many of us have learned to grow through adversity. We have learned to dig up the past and lay it at the feet of the Savior, growing stronger day by day. We may have taken baby steps at first, feeling as awkward as an elephant on ice skates. But we kept going—trusting in the promises of God, relying on His grace and wisdom, and leaning on the strength of our friends—until we discovered genuine joy.

We want you to know that God can bring His healing and help to your situation. We want you to see how you can experience such an inner peace that you can still muster a smile even when life is at its worst.

# ACKNOWLEDGMENTS

Special thanks to the Beacon Hill team: Hardy Weathers, Bonnie Perry, Judi Perry, and Barry Russell. Thanks also to Deloris Leonard for hours of typing and editorial assistance. We also thank Jerry Brecheisen for editorial consultation and creativity and Chonda Pierce for graciously allowing us to use her coined phrase for the title of this book.

STAN TOLER is senior pastor of Trinity Church of the Nazarene in Oklahoma City and for several years taught seminars for Dr. John Maxwell's INJOY Group, a leadership development institute. He serves as the executive director of the Toler Leadership Center located on the campus of Mid-America Christian University and is the cofounder of BGW Forward in Faith. Stan has written more than 70 books, including his best sellers *God Has Never Failed Me, but He's Sure Scared Me to Death a Few Times; The Buzzards are Circling, but God's Not Finished with Me Yet; God Is Never Late; He's Seldom Early; He's Always Right On Time; The Secret Blend; Practical Guide for Pastoral Ministry; Total Quality Life;* and his popular *Minute Motivator* series.

For additional information on seminars, scheduling speaking engagements, or to contact the author:

Stan Toler
P.O. Box 892170
Oklahoma City, OK 73189-2170
E-mail: stoler1107@aol.com
Web site: www.StanToler.com
www.BuildingGodsWay.com

DEBRA WHITE SMITH impacts and entertains readers with her life-changing books, including *Romancing Your Husband; Romancing Your Wife; More Than Rubies: Becoming a Woman of Godly Influence;* the *Jane Austen Fiction series;* and the *Debutantes Series.* She's an award-winning author, including such honors as Top-10 Reader Favorite, Gold Medallion finalist, and Retailer's Choice Award finalist. Debra has written more than 50 books, with more than one million books in print.

The founder of Real Life Ministries, Debra has hosted her own radio show, *Real Life Minute.* She also speaks at ministry events across the nation and has been featured on a variety of media, including *The 700 Club, At Home Life, Getting Together,* Moody Broadcasting Network, Fox News, *Viewpoint,* and *America's Family Coaches.*

Debra lives in small-town America with her husband, two children, and a herd of cats. To contact Debra or schedule speaking engagements:

Real Life Ministries
P.O. Box 1482
Jacksonville, TX 75766
www.debrawhitesmith.com
RealLifeMinistries@suddenlink.net
1.866.211.3400

# 1
# LOOKING GOOD, BUT DYING INSIDE

Then you will know the truth,
and the truth will set you free.
—John 8:32

I (Stan) will never forget the day my father died. My Uncle Roy picked us up in Dad's old '59 Plymouth after school and said, "We need to go to the hospital. Your dad has been hurt in an accident."

Oddly enough, two weeks earlier, I dreamed that my dad had died. Even though it had been only a dream, I awoke shaking from head to toe, sobbing and trying to grasp what life would be like without Dad. When I saw the grim look in my uncle's eyes, I instantly recalled that feeling of panic and distress. Only 11 years old, I had never felt such devastation. Looking back, I think perhaps the Lord was using the dream to prepare me for what lay ahead.

Uncle Roy drove us to Doctor's North Hospital in Columbus, Ohio. My younger brothers and I waited in the car for about five hours while Mom shuttled in and out of the hospital. Finally a policeman came out and told us our dad had passed away. Again I recalled that horrible dream and realized I was actually living the gut-wrenching pain I had only tasted in that nightmare two weeks before. How could I ever go back home knowing Dad wouldn't be there?

When we got home, I didn't even want to get out of the car and go into the house. My heart pounded in despair as my brothers—Terry, age nine, and Mark, age three—sobbed and clung to me in the backseat of the car. Mother was so distraught that Uncle Roy had to help her into the house. I hoped he wouldn't come back; I just wanted to disappear. But in a few moments Uncle Roy returned. At that point I knew I didn't have a choice—I would have to go back into the house.

With my brothers' arms wrapped around me, I started up the steps; but I could go no farther. Gut-wrenching agony overtook me. I collapsed and wailed in pain. I felt as if I were lost, completely lost, on a sea of suffering. Confusion hurled itself upon me. Desperation gripped me. My 11-year-old mind couldn't fathom how this could be. How could Dad—*my dad*—be dead? We had been together just the evening before. I remembered the pleasure of his warm smile. I remembered those father-and-son wrestling matches and his assurance that he loved me with all his might. How could he be dead? *How could he?*

It simply didn't make sense. We had moved to Ohio from West Virginia so Dad wouldn't have to work in the coal mines. He suffered from black lung disease and had broken his back three times before he was 30. He had moved our family to Ohio to make life better. Now he was dead! All our hopes for a better life were gone! I didn't even feel as if we were a family anymore; I wanted to run and hide. I didn't believe I could face the pain I was feeling. Hysterically I cried out, "O God—I can't go into the house again without my daddy!"

Then I heard an almost audible voice—God's voice: "Yea, though I walk through the valley of the shadow of death . . ." (Ps. 23:4, KJV). Immediately I sensed the assurance that I was not alone—the Lord was with me. I stood up, wiped my eyes, and walked into the house on my own. An amazing peace swept over my soul, a peace that gave me the courage to face the difficult days to come.

My temptation had been to hide from pain. Naturally, many of us often shy away from difficult circumstances. But pain can't be hidden forever, and we pay a price when we lock it away in our hearts without facing reality.

## Beeps Anonymous

My (Debra's) friend and fellow writer Frances Shaw discovered the problem with hidden things after a recent move from Dallas back to her hometown of Tyler, Texas. Since Frances is a widow and retiree, my husband, Daniel, and I often help her with household projects.

Frances had been back in Tyler only about three months when she called with a distressing story. There was a strange beeping sound in her house that was driving her *nuts*. At first she thought the smoke alarm was malfunctioning, and she called her landlord. He sent a repairman to check on the problem. After some investigation, the repairman concluded that the smoke alarm was definitely *not* the source of the beep. He then inspected the air conditioner vents and decided that the beep was coming from the attic.

The repairman came back the next day wearing hip boots and carrying his flashlight. With a lighted miner's band around his forehead, he crawled up into the attic. After a futile hour of finding nothing, he concluded that the beep must be coming from the refrigerator. A refrigerator repairman soon arrived to annihilate the tormenting tone. But alas—he, too, failed. After three weeks of suffering the frustrating beep, Frances was beginning to think she might lose her mind.

That's when she called me. I assured her that we would stop by Wednesday night after church and that Daniel, my "mechanical genius," would rid her of the exasperating beep. That night Frances came to the door wringing her hands, eyes glazed with irritation. In the background the faithful beep sounded every few minutes.

Daniel tuned his ears and began walking slowly around the duplex apartment. Amid a host of chuckles, he finally narrowed the noise to the vicinity of a storage closet near the den.

Frances was certain nothing in that storage closet could be beeping. Nevertheless, Daniel opened the closet and began to explore. Finally Frances stumbled upon a crumpled shopping bag that had been left by the former tenant. Slowly she opened the bag—and discovered the source of the beep. Inside the forgotten bag was a spare smoke detector with a spent battery. She rolled with laughter as Daniel removed the battery and forever solved her beep problem.

The next day Frances called the landlord. "Hello—this is Frances," she began with a straight face. "I'm happy to tell you that the beep has stopped." She thanked him politely for his help and then hung up before he could respond.

> With the fearful strain that is
> on me night and day,
> if I did not laugh I should die.
>
> —Abraham Lincoln

Buried emotions have a way of surfacing. Like the beeping smoke detector, pain that's buried will gnaw at the soul. Yet we often mask the pain and suffer in silence. A tragedy strikes. A catastrophe knocks us off our feet, and for years afterward a pathetic cry sounds from the inner closet of our hearts, as tormenting as the forgotten smoke detector. And we will do anything to drown out that cry, even covering it with false laughter. Oddly enough, some of the funniest people are those who have been hurt the greatest. For example, well-known comedian Carol Burnett was raised in a dysfunctional home. She used the mask of humor to cover the aching reminders of her past, just as all of us often do.

## Myths of the Pain Buriers

Christians sometimes hide from pain because they have believed the myths that hover around the church. Believing these false ideas about pain and faith, they choose to hide their pain even from those who care the most about their welfare.

**The first pain-burying myth is that if you are truly faithful to God, you will never experience pain.** Out of the agony of his situation, the Old Testament's Job asked the question, "Have I not wept for those in trouble? Has not my soul grieved for the poor? Yet when I hoped for good, evil came; when I looked for light, then came darkness" (Job 30:25-26). Job seemed to be saying, *Excuse me, God. Did you happen to forget my service on your behalf?* He couldn't understand why the faithful suffer alongside the faithless.

**The second pain-burying myth is that suffering is always a direct result of the sufferer's own sin.** For David, his sin seemed to cause his very joints to ache and his bones to break. He said, "My sin is always before me" (Ps. 51:3). The rebellion of his heart seemed to flesh itself out in physical suffering.

Even though some suffering is the direct result of a specific sin (for example, a drunk driver being paralyzed in an automobile accident), and all suffering is an indirect result of Adam and Eve's sin, not every painful incident should be categorized as a result of unfaithfulness to God.

Scripture clearly banishes such assumptions: "As [Jesus] went along, he saw a man blind from birth. His disciples asked him, 'Rabbi, who sinned, this man or his parents, that he was born blind?' 'Neither this man nor his parents sinned,' said Jesus, 'but this happened so that the work of God might be displayed in his life'" (John 9:1-3).

Those who ignore or try to cover up their pain will become prisoners to it. Only when they acknowledge pain as something that God can use to perfect them and to provide for them can His healing work truly be displayed.

Bruce Larson writes,

> I have an old friend named Ernie who was for many years the pastor of a church in the heart of Baltimore. One Sunday he preached on that well-known text from Romans 8:28: "For we

know that in all things God works for good to those who love him and who are called according to his purpose."

Later, while he stood at the door shaking hands, a man he had not seen before came up, looked him in the eye, and said, "Pastor, do you believe what you were preaching this morning?" Ernie was startled. "I've never been asked that question before," he said. "Let me think about it." But just seconds later, he said, "Yes, yes, I really believe that with all my heart."

The very next day Ernie went duck hunting on Chesapeake Bay with some men from his parish. On the way to the duck blind one of his companions tripped. His shotgun went off and blew out Ernie's eyes. He has been blind ever since.

I met him after that accident. He traveled up and down the East Coast to conferences with his seeing-eye dog. I have never known a man so full of joy and love and faith and optimism than Ernie. On one occasion he told me, "Bruce, my church is in revival. More people are coming, more people are accepting Jesus, and one of the best things is my counseling ministry. I see people who would never come to me if I had sight because they'd be ashamed to be recognized on the street. They can unburden their secret safely with a blind man. My ministry is being blessed because of my blindness."[1]

Assuredly, Ernie's blindness occurred "so that the work of God might be displayed in his life" (John 9:3). While we will never understand why tragedies come our way, we can be certain that God desires to use those tragedies, no matter how devastating, to display His unfailing love and His almighty power. But we must let Him do His work *in His own way.* As long as we focus on the ways God *can* and *should* deliver us, as long as we spend our prayers on bargaining with God, as long as we wail, "What did I do to deserve this?" we will miss seeing His marvelous work displayed in our lives.

### In the Midst of It All

*What have you done to deserve all this?*
*Curse God and die.*

*What advice for a man*
*Who had trusted God most of his life;*
*Then Job speaks as he stands*
*Among a broken down domain,*
*In the midst of it all I shall stand and not fall*
*And bless His name.*

*In the midst of it all . . . in the midst of it all,*
*I've found hope that will never let me fall;*
*Jesus heard my call,*
*And by me stood tall.*
*And in Him I stand complete*
*In the midst of it all.*

*Should the day come when everyone*
*Bows their head to cry,*
*And when man has done all that man can do,*
*And I'm left to die;*
*Well, even then surrounded by affliction's greatest pain,*

*In the midst of it all I shall stand and not fall*
*And bless His name.*
*In the midst of it all . . . in the midst of it all,*
*I've found hope that will never let me fall;*
*Jesus heard my call,*
*And by me stood tall.*
*And in Him I stand complete*
*In the midst of it all.**

—Tim Hill

**The third pain-burying myth is that you're the only one with a problem.** A "soccer mom" was driving the team home from a winning game. The junior athletes packed the Suburban, and they were boisterous to say the least. Distracted by the noise coming from the back of the packed vehicle, Mom didn't see the stop sign.

---

Soon the car with the revolving blue light came into view in the side mirror. Standing by the opened window, the policeman looked at the vanload of kids in the back and then at the driver. "Ma'am, I pulled you over because it looks like you don't know when to stop."

The mother shot back, "And what makes you think all these belong to me?"[2]

That mother wasn't the only one who was having a rough day. Often we choose to cover our pain by trying to convince ourselves that we're the only ones suffering. But the fact is that frustration and pain are a normal part of life—everyone's life. The Bible says, "Man born of woman is of few days and full of trouble" (Job 14:1). In other words, trouble is an element of the human experience.

Before his tragedy, Job was one of those people who seemed to have it all together: wealth, prestige, honor, marriage, family. After his tragedy, after Job surrendered to the plan that God had allowed for his life, God restored him. And once again, the puzzle pieces of his life seemed to fit. The final chapter was filled with peace and wholeness.

Ironically, those who seem the most accomplished and successful are often those who hurt the most. Actor Robert Young, star of *Father Knows Best; Marcus Welby, M.D.;* and more than 100 movies, fought a long battle with depression and alcoholism. He attempted suicide in 1991. Two years later, he stated, "I constantly felt I wasn't worthy, that I had no right to be a star. I hid a black terror behind a cheerful face. Naturally, I tried to find a way out. Alcoholism was the inevitable result."[3]

Young's dilemma could be told and retold with a variety of names and faces. As Patrick Morley puts it, "Sooner or later, we all identify with Job. Few of us will ever suffer the depths that swallowed up his life. The torment which consumed him, and more specifically his response, involuntarily draws us toward him."[4]

While the rest of the world may put up an "all is well" front, Job gives us an honest look at human misery and an accurate view of our human responses. His story shows us this: we are not alone. Believers suffer. Unbelievers suffer. Everyone suffers. Every day we are surrounded by others who are hurting in this journey called life. At this time in history, streets are full of the homeless, Christian parents are devastated by their children's homosexuality, loved ones are dying, earthquakes, tornadoes, hurricanes, unwed mothers, prostitution, orphans. Hurt lines our busy sidewalks.

## Closing the Door

As long as we falsely assume that we are alone in our pain, we close the door on God's ability to heal not only us but others as well. Rest assured—God wants to use our painful experiences to point others to Him. But He won't as long as we erect walls, cover the pain, and bar even Him from access to our grief.

Job not only becomes our journey mate but also proves to us that the destructive plans of Satan himself *can* be defeated. As believers, we do not have to turn to pain-burying attempts such as mind-blurring addictions, mask-covering attitudes, double-duty denial, or anything else. We can declare our faith in the ultimate mercies of God with a holy boldness like Job: "Though he slay me, yet will I hope in him" and "The LORD gave and the LORD has taken away; may the name of the LORD be praised" (Job 13:15; 1:21). We can shout to the enemy with glee, "Take that, devil! You're defeated!"

Again, we are not alone in our pain. Suffering is inevitable for everyone—believers and nonbelievers. Without a doubt, our Heavenly Father longs to turn our tears to sincere laughter—a contagious, overcoming laughter that not only changes us but also brings change to those around us.

> *Give me a sense of humor, Lord;*
> *Give me the grace to see a joke,*
> *To get some happiness from life*
> *And pass it on to other folk.*
>
> —Anonymous

Allen and TaLenda Mulkey stood in the doorway of their Oklahoma City home. The doorway was all that remained in the wake of the devastating tornado that roared through town. The house was flattened, but surprisingly the doorway remained intact. Between tears and laughter, Allen tacked a poster to the door casing. It depicted a sad-eyed beagle with a caption reading, "I know I'm victorious, Lord—but it sure feels like I'm getting stomped."

Granted, experiencing joy in the midst of pain is not an easy assignment. *Knowing* that God is in control of your life is not the same as *feeling* that He is. In those moments of loss and pain, we're tempted to look for God's grace on our terms, not His. We don't want to lose control.

We become like the little boy who went to his mother and announced that he wanted a new bicycle for Christmas. His mother smiled and told him to ask Jesus for it. The little boy went to his room, got out a pencil and a sheet of paper, and began to write: "Dear Jesus, I will be a good boy for an entire day if . . ." He stopped and realized that "an entire day" was too long for him to be good.

So he started writing again: "Dear Jesus, I will be good for an entire hour if . . ." Once again, he stopped. Even an hour was way too long for him to be good!

Just then the boy remembered the statuette of Mary in the family's Christmas Nativity. He went over to it, picked it up, tied a shoelace around its wrists, put it in a box, and hid the box in his closet.

His lips set firmly, he picked up his pencil and began to write again: "Dear Jesus, I just want you to know that I have your mother. If you ever want to see your mama again . . ."

## God, Please Do Something!

Our great desire is for God to *do something* to relieve our pain. We'll bargain, promise, and even threaten in order to get life on our terms. But God doesn't work that way. *We* need to change, not God. He is changeless. Num. 23:19 states, "God is not a man, that he should lie, nor a son of man, that he should change his mind. Does he speak and then not act? Does he promise and not fulfill?"

He is not fickle in His commitments to us. His love and grace toward us are unalterable. Cloudy skies don't bother Him. In fact, the Bible says He *rides* the clouds. We're the ones who are subject to the "partly cloudies." We're the ones who need to make adjustments, and that's never easy.

## God's Grace Helped Me

After my father died, I (Stan) struggled with just about every problem a kid could face: grades, teachers, insecurities, anger, and even resentment toward kids who had a dad at home. But God's grace held me up each step of the way. Even on the nights when I was furious with Him for letting my father die, the Lord was right there to gently assure me and to steer my paths toward righteousness.

My relationship with Christ *grew* in spite of the hurt and pain. Night after night in the silent darkness, I began to meet God. I started leaning on Him as my Father. Ps. 19:14 became my prayer: "May the words of my mouth and the meditation of my heart be pleasing in your sight, O LORD, my Rock and my Redeemer." God ultimately healed my broken heart, filled my life with His joy, and even surprised me with a wonderful gift: a fantastic stepfather who has now been with me longer than my biological father. Today I am a hopeful Christian who can testify to God's healing grace.

So what can you do to move from *masking the pain* to *embracing the joy*? Here are some suggestions.

**Be honest about your hurts.** Jesus said, "You will know the truth, and the truth will set you free" (John 8:32). Christ lovingly beckons you to the "closet" where you have locked away your pain. He wants you to open the "door" of your false attitudes (including that plastic smile) and reveal the contents. Of course, He already knows what's there, but He wants you to confess these attitudes. He wants you to admit your hurts as an act of faith in His healing. And then He wants to hold you while you weep and to whisper His unconditional love to you, helping you experience complete freedom, total joy, and *honest* laughter.

**Thank God for His presence in the midst of the pain.** Suffering is often precisely what draws us closer to God. God's name is often the very first word uttered by an accident victim. Everything else is forgotten. For that brief moment, nothing matters but God. Thank Him for being there in the midst of your pain.

Thank Him also for allowing this classroom of suffering where you will learn more about Him. Thank Him for the lessons you will learn—lessons that will also teach others. Thank Him for the wisdom you will gain as a result of your loss.

**Take refuge in the love of your family.** Let them give you their expressions of affection and affirmation—and give them in return. Express your love for them—even when you don't feel so loving.

Reassure your family that your feelings toward them have not changed, even though everything else has. Confide your fears to them. Let them be your rock of acceptance. In the darkest hour of Jesus' life, as He hung on the Cross, He focused His attention on His mother and made provisions for her welfare. Family mattered to Him even when He was dying.

**Spend some time alone with God.** Find a hideaway from the "noonday heat." Pour out your soul to your Heavenly Father. Take a walk. Time alone, coupled with physical activity, provides the opportunity for refreshing moments of reflection as well as a healthy expending of negative energies. Plan a getaway, a minivacation to one of your favorite places. "Location, location, location" is important in more than real estate. The location you choose for a day away may become a vital reminder of God's presence.

**Spend some time with a close friend.** As Jonathan helped save David's life, so the encouragement of a friend can be the help that will enable you to endure another day. Call a lifelong friend and spend some time reflecting on the "good old days." Share a cup of coffee along with sharing your burdens. Tell a joke or story, and momentarily replace your sadness with gladness.

**Spend some time with a good book.** Bookstores and libraries have Christian literature on subjects that will encourage, uplift, and instruct you in times of trouble. God has allowed many others to go through adversity, and they have penned descriptions of their journey. Learn from them. When the apostle Paul was imprisoned in Rome, he made a request to Timothy, his spiritual son: "When you come, bring the cloak . . . and my scrolls, especially the parchments" (2 Tim. 4:13). Paul knew how important good reading material can be in times of trouble.

**Looking ahead.** You may feel like the man who was so uncertain about the future that he wouldn't buy green bananas. But go ahead—plan for a positive future. Think in terms of the "later on," not just the "now." The writer to the Hebrews said that faith is the substance of things *hoped for*. Regardless of the devastation of the past, remember: "With God all things are possible" (Matt. 19:26). Meditate on the promise of heaven. Think about the things God has prepared for you beyond the events of time. Think about a life free from suffering. God's Word promises that one day "He will wipe away every tear from [our] eyes. There will be no more death or mourning or crying or pain, for the old order of things has passed away" (Rev. 21:4).

**Write it down.** Keep a spiritual journal. Write down the promises God is giving you. Record His words to your spirit. Detail the obvious ways you are being delivered out of your suffering. As songwriter Thomas O. Chisholm wrote, "Morning by morning new mercies I see. / All I have needed Thy hand hath provided. / Great is Thy faithfulness, Lord, unto me!"

**Make an "attitude adjustment."** When a sailor encounters changing winds, an adjustment must be made in the sails to avoid calamity. As you encounter the winds of adversity, you'll have to make adjustments in the sails of your soul. First, you'll have to choose to survive. An overcoming attitude doesn't happen by accident—you must deliberately choose it. God said to the Israelites, "I have set before you life and death, blessings and curses. Now choose life, so that you and your children may live" (Deut. 30:19).

**Minister to others.** Nothing will help you bear the load you are carrying more than helping someone else carry a load. God's Word tells us that we are comforted in times of trouble so that we might comfort others (2 Cor. 1:3-4). For example, why not pray by name for those who need a miracle—maybe even more than you do?

**Reminisce about past blessings, and thank God for His history of faithfulness.** God is always proactive in your life and mine. Think about that, and give Him praise. I (Stan) will never forget my father and the impact he had upon my life. Every Monday morning I get out of bed and take Dad's Timex wristwatch out of my jewelry box. I wind it up and often think of the many good lessons he taught me about life. As usual, I'm wearing this 38-year-old watch as I write these words. Dad was wearing it on the day he was killed. That timepiece was my inheritance as a coal miner's kid.

This watch has never needed repair. It keeps perfect time, and I've replaced the watchband only three times. Certainly it's one of my greatest earthly treasures. Not only is it a symbol of my earthly father's love—it also symbolizes the way my Heavenly Father, *in His time,* can create a melody of joy and healing from pain and sorrow.

My goal in life is to have, if nothing else, emotional resilience. When life smashes me flat, I ask God to give me the courage to joyfully persevere.

—Debra White Smith

# 2
# DOWN, BUT NOT OUT:
## OVERCOMING DEPRESSION

Be merciful to me, O LORD, for I am in distress;
my eyes grow weak with sorrow,
my soul and my body with grief.
—Ps. 31:9

When I (Debra) was 15 years old, my family disintegrated. During that lonely and confused time, I experienced my own personal tragedy. I was sexually abused. I'm convinced that this is one of the most degrading and devastating atrocities anyone can face. Not knowing how to cope with the agony and shame, I chose the only survival strategy that I could see: I locked away my pain.

For more than a decade I buried my torment from my parents' divorce and my sexual abuse. I pretended everything was fine. I worked my way through high school, graduated with honors, began college, married a wonderful man, secured a nice job, and became active at church. The thought of sharing about the sexual abuse was so intensely shameful that I wouldn't even discuss it with my husband. When presented with questions about my family, I put on my strong, happy face for the world. Furthermore, I overachieved at everything I did in an attempt to compensate for my low self-esteem.

## Dealing with the Pain

But when I was about 26, my facade began to crumble. I knew that I had to begin dealing with the pain that I had kept secret for so long. Yet as I started acknowledging those secret hurts, the horror became real all over again. I began to feel the anguish that I had denied for so long. After 11 years of pretending that everything was "normal," I found myself grieving, sobbing, and being depressed over the emotional holocaust I had endured.

One day my husband came home to find me on the bathroom floor weeping uncontrollably. At last, after seven years of marriage, I was able to tearfully confide in him about the abuse I had suffered.

I wasn't prepared for the dark and bitter emotions that followed. I was overcome by wave upon wave of grief over the loss of my family years before. We had had a really good family—not perfect, but good. As I wept oceans of tears, reliving those dark days, I began to fully realize the depth of my loss. I had witnessed a death—the death of our family.

I tread so deeply through depression that there were times when I would have gladly embraced death myself. At that time we lived in a remote area, and my husband kept a gun nearby for our protection. The gun began to beckon me to place the barrel against my temple and pull the trigger. Soon I asked Daniel to remove the gun.

Praise the Lord, I never attempted to take my own life. With God's help, I was able to emerge from those corridors of pain. I regularly beseech Him to continue releasing me from issues of the past and to fill every crevice of my heart with joy. The journey has been difficult, but I can testify to the wonderful truth that there is deliverance from depression.

Many of us have endured the entrapment of depression and have probably asked, *God, are you still up there?* The good news is that He is. Regardless of how we may feel, God is forever "up there," ready and willing to help us break the bonds of depression.

## The Depressed Generation

Depression is the secret plague of our generation. Few are willing to admit it, but many people—including Christians—suffer from depression.

In 1828 Webster's Dictionary defined depression as "the act of pressing down, a slow state. A sinking of the spirits; dejection; a state of sadness; want of courage; a low state of strength."[1] In 1975 Webster's definition of depression was "a psychoneurotic or psychotic disorder marked by sadness, inactivity, difficulty in thinking and concentration, and feelings of dejection. A reduction in activity, amount, quality, or force. A lowering of vitality or functional activity."[2]

The term "age of depression" describes our times. Each recent generation has grown more susceptible to its impact. For example, 1 percent of those born before 1905 had experienced major depression by age 75. In contrast, 6 percent of those born after 1955 have suffered from this condition by age 30. Three percent of men and 6 percent of women will require hospitalization because of severe depression. Furthermore, the rate of depression among men is quickly catching up with the rate of depression among women. It's been estimated that 1 in 10 American adults suffers from some form of depression. In one recent year this malady accounted for 565,000 hospital admissions, 13 million doctor visits, and 7.4 million hospital days.[3]

## Depression Is Nondiscriminatory

Depression does not discriminate in choosing its victims. Wealth and fame are no safeguard against it. For example, on September 8, 1998, Mark McGwire broke the single-season home-run record that had been set by Roger Maris exactly two years to the day before McGwire was born. In the 144th game of the St. Louis Cardinals' 1998 season, the burly first baseman hit his shortest homerun of the season (342 feet) over the left-field fence and secured his place in baseball history. This was one of the greatest accomplishments ever to occur on a baseball diamond—but ironically, the event nearly didn't happen.

After a frustrating season in 1991, when McGwire hit only .201 and was hampered by injuries, he seriously considered retiring. He classified himself as an emotional wreck and thought about giving up. For the next four years he underwent therapy for his depression.

Unlike Mark McGwire, most of us are unwilling to admit that we face emotional pain. Rather than seek treatment, we continue (as I did) to hide the pain.

When facing your emotional needs, honesty is truly the best policy. Are you depressed? Here are some signs.

- Feeling worthless, guilty, helpless, or hopeless
- Having trouble sleeping, or sleeping too much
- Losing appetite or overeating
- Feeling tired, weak, and low on energy
- Feeling restless and unable to sit still
- Having problems concentrating, remembering, or making decisions
- Crying more easily than usual

An assessment of your circumstances might also help to identify depression. Here are some circumstances that can lead to depression:

- Divorce or separation
- Problems with a child: unwanted pregnancy, runaway, homosexuality
- Loss of job
- Problems with finances
- Alcoholism in parent or spouse
- Adultery by spouse
- Incarceration
- Abuse, either sexual, physical, or emotional
- Illness or injury
- Fatigue
- Change of career or address
- Death of a loved one
- Alcohol or drug abuse

By the way, Mark McGwire didn't quit. Seven years after depression brought him to consider leaving baseball, he became "the Sultan of Swat," surpassing the all-time home-run record with 70 round-trippers in the 1998 season. Because he refused to submit to

depression and overcame it, McGwire is a living example to countless people who have been depressed.

> A sense of humor is the pole that adds balance
> to our steps as we walk the tightrope of life.
>
> —William A. Ward

## The Choice Is Ours

There's an old story about a psychologist who counseled a man
who had trouble making decisions. "Mr. Smith," the doctor
queried, "I've been seeing you now for three months. Do you think
we're making any progress? The patient paused for a long time and
then answered, "Well, yes and no."

When facing depression, we must make a choice. We can either
deal with it or cover it up, pretending that all is well. But covering
depression only intensifies the problem. The wisest thing is to follow the example of David, who said, "Why are you downcast, O
my soul? Why so disturbed within me? Put your hope in God, for I
will yet praise him, my Savior and my God" (Ps. 42:5-6). David
made a decision. He determined to bring his condition to the Lord.
And he chose to quit trying to solve the problem in his own
strength. He put his trust in the Almighty for deliverance. That was
a wise choice!

## Moving Beyond Blame

Beating the emotional blues begins with a willingness to admit
you are depressed. The next step is a willingness to trust God.
When faced with confusing, frightening circumstances, blaming is
easier than trusting.

There are times when our blame is misdirected. During a Palm
Sunday service at my father's church, I (Debra) excused myself in
the middle of the sermon for a trip to the ladies' room. When I re-

turned, I smiled at my husband, Daniel, as he turned his legs to one side so I could reclaim my spot beside him on the pew. Stepping in front of his knees, I glanced down at my grandmother, who sat on the pew in front of us, and admired the way the lights shown past her hairnet and onto her smooth hair, turning it almost blue-black.

Carefully, I raised my arm over her head, not wanting to hit her and disturb the rapt attention she bestowed on the minister as he delivered his sermon. Sneaking another lover's smile to my husband, I sat down.

Looking straight toward the pulpit, I had every intention of listening to my father's sermon. But something was wrong with my grandmother.

Her hair!

Why was it standing straight up? Her forever-present hairnet had been keeping it so smooth, so in place. Now her once-neat hair looked like the quills of a porcupine. Every strand stood straight out, reaching for the rafters like cotton candy.

I felt something at my arm. As I glanced down, my confusion grew. My husband slowly, deliberately untangled some black, reticulated thing from the button of my wide, lacy cuff. I wondered if I had somehow snared this strange item in the bathroom.

He leaned toward my ear. "It's her hairnet!" he whispered. His green eyes danced with hilarity.

My grandmother turned around, her dark brown eyes glittering like a mischievous puppy's, her pearly teeth glistening in a special grin just for me. For one split second, the years melted away, and my 80-year-old grandmother turned into a playful teenager—with porcupine hair.

I had often wondered why she never went without the hairnet. Now I knew! Sniffling, laughter tears stinging my eyes, I handed her the soft hairnet in what seemed like a slow-motion replay. Without her gaze meeting mine again, she took it. Her mouth now set in a fiercely determined line, she methodically replaced the hairnet as if she did this sort of thing in every church service.

The porcupine vanished, leaving the smooth blue-black mane in its place. But for me and my husband—and the last half of the congregation—the porcupine didn't go away. It stubbornly hibernated in our minds, blocking out everything else. And I'm guessing no one on those back six pews could remember what my father's sermon was about that Sunday.

As soon as the last "amen" was uttered, a chorus of laughter burst forth in spontaneous release. I didn't think guffaws could get any louder until my grandmother asked very seriously, "Why in the world did Debra rip off my hairnet?"

My poor grandmother actually thought I had done it on purpose!

## Why?

When we're confused and upset by life's circumstances, we often ask the same question: *Why, God? Why did you do this to me?*

Saddened or bewildered by our circumstances, we believe, like my startled grandmother, that God has maliciously inflicted our pain.

Or we may wonder, *Why me? Why am I depressed?* If a person has been truly born of the Spirit, and certainly if he or she has been filled with the Spirit, then shouldn't the blues be gone?

## The Common Commotion

We may wonder, *A depressed Christian? How can that be? Something must be wrong with my spiritual life.*

Not so.

Depression is neither a sign that God is unfaithful nor a sure indication of a spiritual problem. Depression is not only compatible with the Christian experience but actually quite common among believers.

In fact, many of the outstanding characters of the Bible experienced the blues—and even the deep purples. They include Abraham (Gen. 15), Elijah (1 Kings 19), David (1 Sam. 20), and Paul (Acts 9).

Even Christ himself understood despair (Luke 22).

But in spite of these biblical examples, people today who are plagued by depression usually conclude two things: (1) God has forgotten me. (2) I need to handle this on my own.

Yet God has not, and never will, forget His beloved people. David asserts this in Ps. 63:8—"My soul clings to you; your right hand upholds me." Furthermore, God's Word continually reminds us of His unconditional care and love, as in Ps. 107:1, which says, "Give thanks to the LORD, for he is good; his love endures forever." He does care for us. And He watches over us through all of life's heartaches.

## Situations Breed Depression

Many devastating situations in life breed depression, situations that we'll never be able to overcome without God's strength, such as

- Death
- Financial loss
- Illness
- Broken relationships
- Career change

The seeds of sorrow germinate in life's awful conditions. But even there, "He gives strength to the weary and increases the power of the weak. . . . but those who hope in the LORD will renew their strength. They will soar on wings like eagles; they will run and not grow weary, they will walk and not be faint" (Isa. 40:29, 31). Through God's divine strength, we will not only beat the blues but smother them with victory!

> Laughter is a tranquilizer with no side effects.
>
> —Arnold Glasgow

## Overcoming Depression

At a Promise Keepers rally, E. V. Hill told of a Christian lady who lived next door to an atheist man. Every day the atheist heard

~~ing~~. He thought, *She sure is crazy praying all the time*
~~'t~~ *she know there isn't a God?*

~~praying~~ lady ran out of groceries. As usual, she
~~ed~~ to the Lord, explaining her situation and thanking
~~or~~ what He was going to do.

Once more, the atheist heard the lady praying and thought, *Ha!
I'll fix her!* He went to the store, bought a bunch of groceries, and
took them to her house. He placed them on the front porch, rang
the doorbell, and hid in the bushes to see what she would do.

When she opened the door and saw the groceries, she began to
praise the Lord with all her heart, jumping, singing, and shouting
all over the porch.

The atheist then jumped out of the bushes and told her, "You
crazy old lady! God didn't buy you those groceries—I bought them!"

She jumped off the porch and ran down the street, shouting and
praising the Lord. When the man finally caught up with her, he
asked why she was still shouting.

She replied, "I knew the Lord would provide me with some groceries, but I didn't know He was going to make the devil pay for
them!"

In that same way, God wants to turn your despair into joy. He
may even use the circumstances that oppress you as an instrument
of your deliverance.

David outlines this journey in one brief chapter of the Bible, Ps.
13:

> How long, O LORD? Will you forget me forever? How long
> will you hide your face from me? How long must I wrestle with
> my thoughts and every day have sorrow in my heart? How long
> will my enemy triumph over me? Look on me and answer, O
> LORD my God. Give light to my eyes, or I will sleep in death;
> my enemy will say, "I have overcome him," and my foes will re-
> joice when I fall. But I trust in your unfailing love; my heart re-
> joices in your salvation. I will sing to the LORD, for he has been
> good to me.

In this passage, David goes from singing the blues to singing the "Hallelujah Chorus." And so can we!

Let's look at the scriptural sequence:

1. At first, David is in the clutches of despair and seems to be helplessly on his face: "How long, O LORD? Will you forget me forever? How long will you hide your face from me? How long must I wrestle with my thoughts and every day have sorrow in my heart? How long will my enemy triumph over me?" (vv. 1-2).

2. But then David begins to move beyond hopelessness to a new dimension of asking and believing that God can deliver him. Indeed, David starts climbing out of his despair and bowing on his knees: "Look on me and answer, O LORD my God. Give light to my eyes, or I will sleep in death; my enemy will say, 'I have overcome him,' and my foes will rejoice when I fall" (vv. 3-4).

3. Then, from his knees, David moves to his feet to stand victorious before the Lord: "But I trust in your unfailing love; my heart rejoices in your salvation. I will sing to the LORD, for he has been good to me" (vv. 5-6).

Rest assured—God intends for each of us to move from our face to our feet, from darkness to light. He wants us to victoriously overcome. He wants to give us a testimony of His power. He wants us to impact our world for the cause of Christ.

Here are some suggestions for following David's path from despair to joy:

**Talk to a close friend or family member.** First, start talking with God about your despair. Then branch out to include talking with another trusted person. Often God uses the comfort of another human being to begin our journey out of the pits of despair.

**Talk to a trained Christian counselor.** A counselor can't heal you; only God can heal. However, a trained counselor will be able to help you put your situation into perspective and direct you to the right reading material and Bible passages. Have your pastor recommend a qualified counselor.

**Join a local Christian support group.** Being with other individuals who have survived your loss often brings a sense of support in a particular struggle.

**See your doctor.** He or she might be able to pinpoint a physical problem or medication, or other physiological reasons for your depression. The doctor will most likely ask questions such as

"When did you start feeling this way?"

"Have you recently had a major event or change in your life?"

"Have you ever felt this way before?"

"Has anyone in your family ever been diagnosed with depression?"

"Are you taking medications for other problems?"

"Have you thought about suicide?"[4]

**Be cautious about making decisions.** During a time of depression, it's very easy to make unwise decisions involving your family or your finances. Satan often sends a messenger of evil planning to worsen an already bleak situation.

As an added caution, those who are emotionally vulnerable might slip into a relationship that's out of God's will. Be careful to use the Word of God as a guide for all decisions.

**Focus on God, not on your problems.** In *Maybe It's Time to Laugh Again: Experiencing Outrageous Joy,* Charles R. Swindoll features a letter from an individual who is totally focused on problems rather than on God. While reading the following note, be reminded that, with God's help, we can choose our focus:

Dear—

My life stinks! How's the family? I'm okay—really I am—but don't touch me or I'll have to kill you.

As you can probably tell from the preceding, everything is pretty normal around here. The central air in our house doesn't work; the car is hanging on, having only required a $250.00 clutch/brake job; the washing machine fell apart; the hard drive on my PC crashed (and burned); the door fell off the dishwasher; and we have a hot water leak (you can hear it running, but we can't find it). That is just in the last month. We have other exciting stories, dealing mostly with money, that I won't bore you with. I know someone's bound to have it worse than me . . . but occasionally I think Job had it easy.[5]

**Remember that it takes time to overcome depression.** This is especially true when grieving a loss. The events that brought you loss may have happened suddenly. But the effects of the loss may present lingering and long-term effects. Cures for our emotional hurts often take time. Even if the pain, sorrow, and depression have not passed quickly, the Lord is more than ready, and forever able, to hold us and help us during the longer-term recovery process.

**Acknowledge that you're depressed.** Admitting your need is a vital step toward your healing.

**Pray for God to deliver you from your depression.** James 5:16 says, "The prayer of a righteous man is powerful and effective."

**Claim Jer. 29:11-13 as life verses.** "'I know the plans I have for you,' declares the LORD, 'plans to prosper you and not to harm you, plans to give you hope and a future. Then you will call upon me and come and pray to me, and I will listen to you. You will seek me and find me when you seek me with all your heart'" (Jer. 29:11-13).

**Maintain your life goals.** Don't give up now! Work toward completion.

**Set aside additional time for rest.** In the stress and busyness of Jesus' earthly ministry, He suddenly announced to His disciples, "Come with me by yourselves to a quiet place and get some rest" (Mark 6:31). The Master understood the importance of His disciples to recharge their emotional batteries.

**Focus on the positive power of a relationship with Jesus Christ.** The apostle Paul said, "My God will meet all your needs according to his glorious riches in Christ Jesus" (Phil. 4:19). Faith in Jesus Christ is not only a source of strength but also a source of peace.

## Times of Loss

During times of loss, depression is nearly inevitable. A Sunday School teacher read the Scripture verse to her class in which Jesus said, "My yoke is easy" (Matt. 11:30). Then she asked, "Class, what is the 'yoke' that God puts on us?"

The little girl in the front row raised her hand and spoke at the same time: "Teacher, I know!"

"What is it?" the teacher responded.

"It's when God puts His arm around your shoulder and takes you for a walk."[6]

God wants to put His arm around us and walk us through our times of despair. If we're willing to wait patiently before Him, He'll put a new song in our hearts. "I waited patiently for the LORD; he turned to me and heard my cry. He lifted me out of the slimy pit, out of the mud and mire; he set my feet on a rock and gave me a firm place to stand. He put a new song in my mouth, a hymn of praise to our God. Many will see and fear and put their trust in the LORD" (Ps. 40:1-3).

### Mourning Dawns

Mourning dawns.
The sun is breaking the eastern sky.
The birds of heaven sing and fly.
My saddened heart longs for joy,
Cries for the morning, to end this ploy.
My eyes rove upward, past tree and star,
Past all the burdens that heavy are.
Can God still be there, can He still see
This pain, this loss that torments me?
His presence fills me, soft and dear.
Yes, I see. I know. I'm here.
Your pain is Mine. Your sorrow I feel.
Your loss isn't yours alone, but Mine as well.
I'll carry you through. I'll be your friend
Until your hard journey is at end.
I wilt in His arms. I cling to His breast.
He's there for me. He's there and I rest.
The pain isn't gone. The sorrow's not past.

But His presence alone will bear them at last.
—Debra White Smith

## How to Help Someone Who Is Depressed

A short time ago I (Stan) received word that a good friend of mine had taken his own life. He had endured serious depression for more than 10 years, and no one outside his family ever knew.

The cause of his depression was linked to the loss of several family members all within a few years. He was the kind of person who always seemed "up" and laughed a lot. I was shocked beyond words to learn that he had killed himself, and I couldn't stop thinking of how "together" my friend had seemed.

We must also be sensitive to the emotional needs of our friends and loved ones. It would be good to ask the Lord to help us in this area. His Holy Spirit will be faithful to reveal the needs of the hurting. Some of the signs of despair in our own lives are clues that can be seen in the lives of others.

Depression may not be your problem. But it may affect someone close to you. I sorely wish that I had realized my friend's need and had been able to reach out to him in some way.

My own brother, Mark Toler-Hollingsworth, overcame a serious bout with depression. Reflecting on his healing, Mark has identified several steps that anyone can take to help a person who is depressed.

**Be there.** You have to be present to win! You don't have to say a lot. In fact, those who are depressed are not good conversationalists. Don't ask a lot of questions. Depressed folks have enough questions without trying to answer yours too. You are there to listen, to help your friend vent his or her frustrations and doubts, and to provide a spirit of encouragement.

I love the classic story of the little girl whose neighbor had lost her only son to a terrible illness. "I'm going next door to help Mrs. Williams," the little girl announced to her mother.

Later, after her return, the mother asked if she had helped her grieving neighbor. "Sure did," the girl replied.

"And how did you help her?" her mother asked.

"I went over by the chair where she was sitting, took her by the hand, and just cried with her."

**Don't preach.** The last thing a depressed person needs is a sermon. However, sharing an uplifting scripture may be appropriate. During Mark's period of depression, one of his church members stopped by the house unannounced. At that moment the last thing on earth he wanted to do was to be with people. And he certainly didn't need anyone telling him to "just trust in the Lord."

But what that member did was get out of the car, come over to Mark, hug his neck, tell him that he was loved, and hand him a gift—a beautiful blanket with the words of Jesus, "Come unto me, all ye that labour . . . and I will give you rest" (Matt. 11:28, KJV). Mark sobbed for hours as he thought of that loving gift.

**Love the person unconditionally.** Depressed people often are incapable of loving themselves. They can't comprehend how anyone else, including God, would love them. Expressions of love and affection, either verbal or written, are important to those who are recovering from depression. They need to know they will not be abandoned regardless of their emotional condition.

**Encourage the depressed person.** Sometimes we have to have faith not only for ourselves but also enough for others. Let your depressed friend know how much you believe in him or her. Reinforce his or her good qualities. Remind the person of his or her strengths.

Don't be like the psychiatrist who told a patient struggling with feelings of inferiority, "I've been studying your case, and I've come to the conclusion that you really are inferior!"

**Try to engage the depressed person in activity.** Don't give him or her a choice. Call on the spur of the moment and say, "We're going fishing—I'll meet you." or "Let's have lunch—I'll pick you up in 30 minutes." Don't give the depressed person time to think about whether or not he or she can participate in an activity. If you give him or her a choice, it'll be "No!" every time.

**Pray with the depressed person.** When Mark went through a time of depression, he was frustrated because he just couldn't bring himself to pray. For 16 years of pastoral ministry, people had called upon him to pray for them. "Now," he says, "I didn't even have enough spiritual strength to ask God to bless my Honey Nut Cheerios."

You have made known to me the path of life;
you will fill me with joy in your presence,
with eternal pleasures at your right hand.

—Ps. 16:11

## Understand the Process

Healing usually doesn't happen in a single moment. It is a continuing process—with some valleys as well as mountaintops along the way.

For instance, at the age of 48 on an airplane from London, I (Stan) wept through the movie *October Sky.* This stirring film depicts the life of coal miners and brought back memories of my deceased father.

There is no quick-and-easy remedy for recovery. But as you are willing to follow David's example in turning to God, and as you apply the life principles of those who have survived (and continue to survive), you'll continue to find strength for your journey. And you'll rediscover the faithfulness of a loving God.

The Bible speaks of a time when all tears shall be
wiped away. But it makes no mention of a time
when we shall cease to smile.

—J. D. Eppinga

# 3
# GETTING PAST
# THE PAST

Forgetting what is behind and straining
toward what is ahead, I press on toward
the goal to win the prize for which God
has called me heavenward in Christ Jesus.
—Phil. 3:13-14

Jack becomes hysterical at the sight of water. Whenever something happens to the plumbing in his home, even the slightest drip of a faucet, he begins to hyperventilate. It all goes back to that one spring Saturday morning over a decade ago when he decided to tackle a small household plumbing job.

Jack had just gotten up and was making his way blindly to the kitchen to start some coffee. On the way, he ran into his wife, still in her nightgown, who uttered those 11 fateful words, "Do you think you could fix the leak in the bathroom?" (A question that should be posed only in the strongest of marriages.)

"Sure thing," he muttered. "I'll be back in a minute."

Without stopping at the coffeemaker, Jack, still in his Fruit Of The Looms, went straight to the cabinet and pulled out his "complete set of plumbing tools"—one pair of pliers, a flathead screwdriver, and a hammer.

As Jack began to work on the faucet, he figured that if anything went wrong, he would simply reach under the sink and shut off the water source. Obviously, he had neither read Murphy's Laws nor fixed a dripping faucet.

He successfully removed the knob on the hot water faucet and began unscrewing the center of the mechanism underneath the sink. When the last thread of the screw released its final hold against the hot water behind it, "Old Faithful" erupted right there in the bathroom!

The water pressure shot the screw toward Jack's left eye at 150 feet per second. Fortunately, he wasn't watching what he was doing, so the screw missed his eye, lodging harmlessly in the ceiling. But the geyser of scalding water that followed was doing major damage to the textured ceiling surface above his head.

Frantically, Jack looked under the sink. *No shutoff valve!* He searched again. Still nothing! That's when he spotted the trash can. He quickly heaved the trash into the hallway without looking where he was throwing it, inverted the can, placed it over the shooting water, and redirected the geyser into the sink.

His wife, Lisa, who had been standing in the doorway, was now wearing last week's trash as an accent to her lovely nightgown. Through years of marriage she had learned that the best way to irritate her husband was to act serene when he was completely hysterical. "What happened, Dear?" she asked innocently.

"Hold this!" Jack shouted, pointing at the garbage can. "I'm going to get Sam next door. Maybe he knows where the shutoff valve is."

Within a minute, Sam, who was not fully awake himself, came in to seek the elusive valve. *Still no valve!* Infected by Jack's hysteria, Sam ran toward the front door, heading for the main valve in the front yard.

Unfortunately, he didn't see the pristine storm door looming straight ahead.

Sam ran right through it, sending thousands of pieces of glass all over the porch, except, of course, for the 50 or 60 small shards that were now embedded in his arms and legs.

Meanwhile, Billy—Jack and Lisa's five-year-old, who had seen a special program on violent storms the night before—knew exactly what he was witnessing. "Tornado!" he shouted.

Clad only in his baby briefs, he began circling the living room like a hysterical vulture, screaming at the top of his tiny lungs, "Tornado! Tornado!"

Finally, after shutting off the main valve, picking all the glass out of Sam's Swiss-cheese-like skin, and calming Billy down with a nice dose of cough syrup, Jack and Lisa restored order.

Eight hours later, they had a new storm door (courtesy of Sam); a newly painted, texture-free ceiling (courtesy of Jack); and a non-drip hot water faucet (courtesy of a 10-cent rubber washer).

That's why to this very day Jack gets a sick feeling whenever he sees a dripping faucet.[1]

## Facing the Past

The past can have a powerful effect on our lives—like an out-of-control water faucet. Similar to Jack, we can be hysterical over past failures, becoming their virtual prisoners. Try as we might, we can't get past that "Old Faithful" moment, when life went crazy.

Perhaps before we knew the Lord, when Satan had his grip on us, we did some things that were sinful, disgusting, embarrassing. Or perhaps Satan had a hold on someone else who victimized us. Whatever the case, we all have a past, and Satan wants to keep us bound to it for our entire lives. He delights when we're forever nervous about "dripping faucets" or living in defeat because of what happened years ago.

## God Wants Us to Move Forward

Bondage to the past is not God's plan for us. He wants us to move forward. He yearns to help us put the past *in* the past. He desires that we use our victorious walk with Him as a testimony of His mighty power and deliverance.

In John 8:2-11, a tragic, sinful past unfolds in the dramatic story of a woman caught in adultery. The cast consists of Jesus, the adulterous woman, and a circle of condemning leaders.

During the wee hours of the morning, the woman had been dragged barefoot and disheveled from the bed of a man who was not her husband. Now she stands before the Temple crowd, and the question of life or death is posed before Jesus. The Law states that the punishment for adultery is death. In an effort to embarrass Jesus, the leaders ask Him to decide the woman's fate.

As He did so often, Jesus disappoints the hypocritical leaders by refusing to enter into a debate. Instead, He simply stoops down and gathers His thoughts.

The crowd waits.

The silence is deafening.

He writes in the sand with His finger.

The bystanders crane their necks to decipher what He's writing.

Those words still remain a mystery. Some have suggested He just doodled in the sand to keep His composure in the face of such hypocrites. Others contend that He was quoting Moses. Still others have argued that He was starting to list names. A glance to the left, another to the right—maybe He was writing the names of the prominent leaders in "condemnation's circle."

Finally, Jesus stands up.

Time and again, Jesus has shown compassion for sinners—and yet, the Law of Moses is uncompromising in its treatment of sinners. Have they successfully driven a wedge between the Master's loyalty to the Law and His love for sinners?

When they continue to question Him, Jesus looks them in the eye and says, "If any one of you is without sin, let him be the first to throw a stone at her." Again, He stoops down and writes on the ground.

One by one the stones fall from the hands of the angry crowd. One by one, starting with the oldest, the "circle of condemnation" disbands.

They're alone now—the wise Teacher and the adulterous pupil, the Lawgiver and the lawbreaker. Jesus turns to her and asks, "Woman, where are they? Has no one condemned you?"

The words stumble from her embarrassed, timid lips: "No one, sir."

"Then neither do I condemn you," Jesus declares. And then He utters the eight most freeing words in all of Scripture: "Go now and leave your life of sin" (John 8:7, 10-11).

*Get past your past!*

Jesus gave that woman the freedom to rise above her failures and to face the future.

Only when we get *past our past* can the Lord use us to our full potential. Everyone has lived through a time when, for one reason or another, he or she did not follow the laws of God. All of us at one time have chosen the paths of sin. Some have been victimized by the sins of others. The adulterous woman actually represents both. Not only was she a sinner, but she was also a victim, misused by the religious leaders. Whether we commit sin or it is committed against us, it always produces sorrow—always.

## Battling the Past

People often choose to deal with their past in unhealthful ways. The very first people to deal with a haunting history have become poster children for that dysfunction.

Adam and Eve were guilty of sin—ashamed, embarrassed, trapped by the consequences of their own actions. How did they deal with their situation? With

> *denial,*
> *blaming others,*
> *excuse-making,*
> *rationalizing.*

Too often we follow their poor example.

**Denial** can come in the form of locking away the pain of bad experiences in a dark closet of our heart. Or it can take the form of trying to hide the fact that we have indeed sinned and caused harm to others. This is exactly what Adam and Eve did in Gen. 3. They hid from God. The hiding resulted in a cycle of dysfunction—including dysfunctional relationships. Unconfessed sin will mar every area of our lives.

**Blaming** others represents another nasty cycle. If we have been victims, a perpetual mind-set of blame will eventually lead us to bitterness and an unforgiving spirit. If we have been perpetrators instead of taking responsibility for our misdeeds, we often point our fingers at everyone else. When confronted with their sinful actions, Adam blamed Eve, and Eve pointed to the serpent. Our society passes blame as Olympic runners pass the baton.

We have a human tendency to repeat the sins of our fathers and mothers and then say, "Well, my father [mother] taught me this sin by his [her] example, so it's *his [her]* fault."

But God has given us a moral choice. Regardless of what our parents did or did not do, another person's sin never justifies our own.

**Excuse-making** usually sounds something like, "Oh, that wasn't so bad, Lord—other people are doing it." And we snicker like a little child who lied about eating forbidden cookies. We try to hide the shame.

However, the Lord knows that often "the harder we laugh, the deeper we hurt" and that only His forgiveness and healing in the corridors of our heart will give us freedom from the past.

Our excuses for past sins usually stem from deception. We try to convince ourselves with some semblance of truth—often embarrassingly. For instance, Adam's "I heard you in the garden, and I was afraid because I was naked; so I hid" (Gen. 3:10) sounded believable. But the actual truth is he had eaten from the tree of knowledge of good and evil and was hiding because of his disobedience. Sure, he knew he was naked, but God had seen him naked since He created him! More significantly, Adam was *ashamed,* and this shame came from his disobedience.

A computer engineer ran into his supervisor's office. "I've done it!" he shouted.

"Done what?" The supervisor asked.

He replied excitedly, "I've invented the greatest laptop computer in the world!"

"Wow!" The supervisor exclaimed. "And what makes you think it's the greatest laptop in the world?"

He continued, "Because, when it malfunctions, the error message blames another computer!"

That's just like us. We're so human, we're almost *computers!*

God lovingly confronts us with an unconfessed sin in our past, and we say something like, "Well, Lord, you know . . . um . . . it was so much easier to just give in. It seemed to be the thing to do. Besides, all I did was react to another person's sin." But as long as we make excuses, we won't be making any spiritual progress in being freed from our past.

**Rationalizing** is a fourth unhealthful way of dealing with the past. This usually takes the form of trying to rewrite God's laws. For instance, we may develop the notion that certain sins are wrong *most* of the time instead of all of the time or that God really didn't mean that we were to *always* abstain from a certain attitude or action—or that those sins in our past are just a time in our lives that God has covered with a blanket of understanding. That's Satan's trap—a trap he used on Eve when he asked her, "'Did God really say, "You must not eat from any tree in the garden?"'"

"The woman said to the serpent, 'We may eat fruit from the trees in the garden, but God did say, "You must not eat fruit from the tree that is in the middle of the garden, and you must not touch it, or you will die."'"

"'You will not surely die,' the serpent said to the woman. 'For God knows that when you eat of it your eyes will be opened, and you will be like God, knowing good and evil'" (Gen. 3:1-5).

Such a rationalization of sin never brings healing from the past.

An equally tragic rationalization sometimes occurs when we have been victims of someone else's sin. In need of emotional and spiritual deliverance, we live in emotional agony our whole lives, believing Satan's lies about God's healing.

But God *is* a God of deliverance. And that deliverance includes all of our past—including our sinful lifestyles as well as our past pain. Jesus said, "The Spirit of the Lord is on me, because he has anointed me to preach good news to the poor. He has sent me to proclaim freedom for the prisoners and recovery of sight for the blind, to release the oppressed, to proclaim the year of the Lord's favor" (Luke 4:18-19).

## "The Cross Is History!"

For those of us who have undergone emotional holocaust, Satan would have us believe that Christ's death on the Cross really has no present-day effect. "It's history," he tells us. But nothing could be farther from the truth. The One who is "the same yesterday and today and forever" (Heb. 13:8) is our present-day Deliverer.

This "history" is *His* story! The blood of His forgiveness still flows—and it is a healing flow (see 1 John 1:9).

Once we stop *denying, blaming, excusing,* and *rationalizing,* God will bring us to a place where we can place our trust in Him for healing. He will lovingly confront us with our sin, and He will give us an opportunity to express our sorrow for disobeying Him.

And then He will open His arms of acceptance and forgiveness.

He will cast our past failures into the vast ocean of His forgiveness, where they will be lost forever. Only after facing the past in that way can we do what Jesus told the adulterous woman to do: *Get past your past.*

### Hurt by Hurt

*Nobody saw it, nobody noticed,*
*just how it started.*
*Wounds that were silent, wordless and cruel,*
*tore me apart.*
*And nobody saw how I died;*
*died inch by inch on the inside.*

*Hurt by hurt, the painful mem'ries*
*waited in line.*
*Hurt by hurt, I built the wall*
*one hurt at a time.*

*Gentle as raindrops, welcome as morning,*
*after the darkness.*
*Without a warning, love broke right through,*
*invading my heart.*
*You walked hurt by hurt through my past;*
*and melted barriers at last.*

*Hurt by hurt, the painful mem'ries*
*waited in line.*
*Hurt by hurt, You healed them all*
*One hurt at a time.*

*I praise Your name,*
*and I'm so glad You came.*
*O Jesus, where would I be without You?*
*You knew!*

*Hurt by hurt, the painful mem'ries*
*waiting in line.*
*Hurt by hurt, You heal them all*
*one hurt at a time.*
*Lord, heal them all . . . one hurt . . . at a time.\**
—Gloria Gaither

## Warning! Explosive Past Ahead

There's an old saying that those who don't learn from the past are doomed to repeat it. It's true that past experiences can powerfully affect the future.

---

\*"Hurt by Hurt," music by William Gaither and J. D. Miller. © Copyright 1987 Gaither Music Company, Shepherd's Fold Music. All rights reserved. Words used by permission.

When the Toler family moved from West Virginia to Ohio, we experienced many changes. Not only did we have indoor plumbing for the first time, but instead of having a coal stove for cooking, we had a gas stove with an oven.

We were uptown!

We hadn't been in Ohio long when Mom excitedly went to the grocery store and purchased a canned ham. She read the instructions, preheated the oven to 425 degrees, and placed the canned ham in the oven—can and all!

Mom smiled sweetly and said, "Off we go to church; our ham will be ready when we get back!"

After church we hurried home, looking forward to eating our oven-roasted ham. To our dismay, we discovered that our canned ham was just a bit "overcooked." In fact, it had exploded in the oven, blown off the oven door, and sent most of the ham to the ceiling![2]

Unresolved, hidden wounds from the past are like that canned ham in the oven. Sooner or later, they'll explode. If we don't break free from the past, it will eventually destroy our present and our future—along with our emotional health, our very quality of life. Like the ham in the oven, a past left tightly sealed within our hearts will ultimately detonate and wreak havoc in our souls.

The challenge of facing a potentially explosive past and asking God to free us takes courage. C. Neil Strait observes that "change is always hard for the man who is in a rut. For he has scaled down his living to that which he can handle comfortably and welcomes no change—or challenge—that would lift him."

If we have lived year after year in the bondage, or ruts, of our pasts, then allowing the Lord to free us might easily prove to be the most challenging journey of our life. But we must take the trip if we are to know spiritual victory.

In order to break free from the bondage of the past, we must move out of the ruts of harmful thoughts and actions. How? Consider these steps:

**Confess your sins to God.** To confess your sin is to agree with God concerning its severity. King David said, "Against you, you only, have I sinned and done what is evil in your sight, so that you are proved right when you speak and justified when you judge" (Ps. 51:4). Attitudes and actions that are contrary to God's law must be admitted spiritually.

"I'm guilty, your honor," the offender is heard to say. And the same expression heard in an earthly court of law must be expressed before the courts of heaven. *I'm guilty, Lord. I have sinned against you. And I'm sorry enough for my actions to stop doing them.*

This is the secret of spiritual victory. "This is what the Sovereign LORD, the Holy One of Israel, says: 'In repentance and rest is your salvation, in quietness and trust is your strength'" (Isa. 30:15).

**Set the record straight.** "If you are offering your gift at the altar and there remember that your brother has something against you, leave your gift there in front of the altar. First go and be reconciled to your brother; then come and offer your gift" (Matt. 5:23-24).

"Do what you can, and God will do the rest." God gives His peace to those who actively seek it while doing their very best. And those actions may include going to an individual and confessing harbored resentments against his or her actions.

**Give your past to God.** "Forget the former things; do not dwell on the past. See, I am doing a new thing! Now it springs up; do you not perceive it? I am making a way in the desert and streams in the wasteland" (Isa. 43:18-19).

John Wesley suggested that we can't do much about the birds of temptation flying over our heads, but we don't have to let them make nests in our hair. We can proactively focus on our forgiveness rather than our failures.

**Think about your future in Christ.** "Not that I have already obtained all this, or have already been made perfect, but I press on to take hold of that for which Christ Jesus took hold of me. Brothers, I do not consider myself yet to have taken hold of it. But one thing I do: Forgetting what is behind and straining toward what is ahead, I press on toward the goal to win the prize for which God has called me heavenward in Christ Jesus" (Phil. 3:12-14).

We may have suffered the very worst, but through faith in Christ, the best is yet to come.

When we became children of God by inviting the Lord Jesus Christ into our hearts, He brought with Him a glorious hope—a hope greater than any horror that we have seen or endured.

**Enjoy God's forgiveness.** "Then behold, they brought to Him a paralytic lying on a bed. When Jesus saw their faith, He said to the paralytic, 'Son, be of good cheer; your sins are forgiven you'" (Matt. 9:2, NKJV).

Notice that Jesus' declaration was in the present perfect tense: *"are* forgiven" (emphasis added). God's forgiveness isn't something we earn by degree—it is something that is ours *by His declaration.* No single incident in our past is excluded from His grace.

**Obediently walk in the light of God's Word.** "If we walk in the light, as he is in the light, we have fellowship with one another, and the blood of Jesus, his Son, purifies us from all sin" (1 John 1:7).

Reading God's Word every day is like a daily reading of our personal emancipation proclamation. The rights of our spiritual freedom from past failure are specifically spelled out.

**Communicate** your newly found freedom with friends and family. Throughout the New Testament, people who have been touched by the healing and forgiveness of Jesus are seen going back to their families and friends to tell what happened to them.

"A man with leprosy came to him and begged him on his knees, 'If you are willing, you can make me clean.' Filled with compassion, Jesus reached out his hand and touched the man. 'I am willing,' he said. 'Be clean!' Immediately the leprosy left him and he was cured" (Mark 1:40-42). Jesus instructed the healed man to say nothing to anyone else before he reported to the Temple priests and offered a sacrifice according to the Mosaic Law.

But what was the healed man's reaction? "Instead he went out and began to talk freely, spreading the news" (v. 45).

**Connect** to an encourager. One of the first-century disciples of Jesus was a man named Joseph. The other disciples gave him a nickname that stuck: "Barnabas," which means "Son of Encouragement." Barnabas was known for his encouraging spirit.

Once God has freed you from your past by His forgiveness, seek out the counsel and support of a fellow believer. That bond of fellowship and accountability will reinforce the work the Lord has done in your life.

**Praise God** for His overcoming power. "I lift up my eyes to the hills—where does my help come from? My help comes from the LORD, the Maker of heaven and earth. He will not let your foot slip—he who watches over you will not slumber; indeed, he who watches over Israel will neither slumber nor sleep. The LORD watches over you—the LORD is your shade at your right hand; the sun will not harm you by day, nor the moon by night. The LORD will keep you from all harm—he will watch over your life; the LORD will watch over your coming and going both now and forevermore" (Ps. 121:1-8).

David was expressing praise to God on behalf of the Israelites. In doing so, he was thanking God for His deliverance. Praise is not only an expression of thanksgiving but also an expression of trust for future deliverance.

### Forgiven

> *I'm amazed at how quickly He forgot*
> *All the sin and the wrong I had brought*
> *To the cross of Calvary*
> *When His blood was shed for me.*
> *I'm amazed that it covers every sin.*
> *Yes, I'm amazed at how quickly He forgot.**
> —Terry Toler

---

*© 2000 by Terry Toler Publishing (administered by Integrated Copyright Services, Nashville, Tennessee). Used by permission.

## Freed at Last: Triumph over a Dark Past

When he was five, my son Seth was asked to pray before I
(Stan) got onto an airplane in Oklahoma City. He bowed his head,
folded his hands, and prayed, *Dear Lord, please watch over my daddy. You know Delta, and all their plane crashes!*

As an experienced flyer, I know that my son's description of that
fine air carrier was an exaggeration. Nobody wants to have a reputation for bad crashes. That's why some Christians are reluctant to
share their story of deliverance from the past. They dread what fellow Christians might say if they knew about their former lives—
their crashes. However, often the reaction to the accounts of God's
deliverance is gratitude and praise. Many Christians are more apt to
"rejoice with those who rejoice" (Rom. 12:15).

God wants to break all the chains that bind us—the bondage of
the past as well as slavery to the opinions of others. This freedom
enables us to be transparent before others and before God. And
God wants us to be loving and forgiving of one another. "Forgive,"
the Scripture teaches, "as the Lord forgave you."

But Christians are human, and sometimes they react in a very
human way. A friend of mine (Debra's) was delivered from a shameful past. She made some choices against God's divine plan during
her late teens and early 20s. However, she experienced the Lord's
complete and miraculous deliverance from a life of sin.

Naive in her youth, she assumed that most Christians would
love to hear her story and rejoice with her over her deliverance. But
she soon learned differently.

In the following letter to her parents, she details her own struggles for deliverance, not only from sin but also from the fear of
what other believers will think or do to her once they learn of her
wrong choices.

Dear Mom and Dad,

I am writing because I want to share some things with you
about myself that the Lord has been dealing with me about.
Three weeks ago, our pastor was preaching a series of messages

on fear. On this Sunday morning, God stirred my heart about a fear—really the only fear—that I had. I moved to the altar to ask God to help me . . . to deliver me from this fear that had gripped me for many, many years.

I spent the week burdened about it, and the next Sunday night, while sitting in church, the Lord reached out to me and touched me and said, "I release you from your fear." I looked deep within myself and realized the fear really was gone. As my heart was pounding with this realization, God asked me to be willing to stand before the people of my church and testify about what He had done for me. I told Him that I would, and a week later, on a Sunday night, I stood and testified to my church body and claimed my deliverance from this fear. Now, I want to share this with you.

I know that some of this will be uncomfortable for you. I pray that this won't cause you to feel the need to withdraw from me in any way, but if that is what you are left feeling, then I will wait for you as you process this and find your comfort.

I was very well loved by both of you growing up. I would also say that I was very strongly protected from life. While that kept me from many things that the world had to offer and was your best effort at keeping me from error, I found myself very naive. I was somewhat clueless as to how sin would approach me in life and didn't have a working knowledge of how to resist evil. I knew how to be a good girl . . . how to do whatever I was told and not mess up. That kept peace in the house, and I wanted that very much. But I felt that if I ever really behaved in a way that shamed you, my actions would be unforgivable. It was with these life experiences and emotions that I entered into the period of my life that follows.

Mom, you once asked me, at the end of my senior year of high school, whether or not my relationship with a girl named Monica was appropriate. I assured you that it was, but that was a lie. To be honest, I never clearly noticed when she stepped over the line of a natural appropriate friendship into something inappropriate. I found myself enjoying her company and just watching this unfold before me. Somehow, in my naïveté I didn't perceive it as some blatant sin. When you asked me about the relationship, that was the first time I sensed that I should fear it, and that startling realization caused me to lie to you. However, I also immediately ended the relationship.

The next time Monica came to visit me, I told her that our relationship was wrong and that it must end. She quickly agreed with me. We prayed and cried together as we allowed our alliance to die.

Some time later, while home on a college break, Monica came to see me and invited me to spend a weekend with her at her mother's house. When I returned from the weekend away, Dad met me with a stern warning to meet him the next morning before work. Dad, you were very angry. I showed up for our meeting, and you were upset because I had gone to Monica's mother's.

Eventually you got around to accusing me of an inappropriate relationship. I immediately denied the claim, which was truthful of the current friendship, but you wouldn't hear me. Looking back, I can see why you may have resisted my denial if you sensed earlier that things might have been inappropriate. But on that day, knowing what I had settled months before, I could only feel horrible mistrust. And I couldn't possibly tell you the absolute truth. I truly feared that this truth would be the one thing that would get me removed from the family. I had no confidence that you would love me unconditionally.

I went away to college and spent a couple of great years unhindered by homosexuality. Then a girl showed up out of nowhere who had little Christian influence in her life. One night she confided to me that she had struggled with homosexuality. I could only think of how glad I was that I could encourage her—that she could walk away and God would help her.

But when I told her that I understood those feelings, she became a roaring lion in my life. She couldn't hear my encouragement to be set free. She just saw me as a target, as a prey to be hunted. I fought hard to keep her away, but I just didn't have a working knowledge on how to defeat the devil at his own game. Eventually I gave in. It never crossed my mind that I should invite help from authorities. I trusted no one with this information. At the end of that school year, I got as far away from her as I could and prayed she wouldn't show up again.

Over the next couple of years in college, the devil kept a steady stream of opportunities before me. I didn't always do the right thing. I was by no means free. I was a perfect example of how sins against the flesh are far worse to overcome. In fact, the first verse of "Love Lifted Me" described me perfectly:

> *I was sinking deep in sin,*
> *Far from the peaceful shore,*
> *Very deeply stained within,*
> *Sinking to rise no more.*

I recognized that I was either going to drown from the choking lies of Satan and give up the battle all together, or I was going to have to plant my feet on the Word of God and claw my way to the surface. I knew that if I would renounce sin and begin denying myself, God would respect that and meet me every step along the way. The battle was agonizing.

I have heard every excuse the devil has to offer. I know how he works. But I am living proof that he needn't win. There were times that I thought I would surely physically die from the agony of the battle, but here's where the rest of "Love Lifted Me" comes in:

> *But the Master of the sea*
> *Heard my despairing cry—*
> *From the waters lifted me;*
> *Now safe am I.*

Truly, love lifted me, and for the past 15 years I have led a righteous and pure life before the Lord. I learned never to turn around or look back and gaze upon what I had lost. The story of Lot and his family leaving Sodom with only one restriction, that they not turn around, grips me. If they turned around, it would mean that they longed for the familiar—those things that God despises—and that they were resistant to God's justice. The Lord cautioned me one day not to stop and ponder what was behind me, but to keep my face toward Him. That would be my deliverance.

What, you may ask, does this have to do with the fear I mentioned at the beginning? After I gave all of that up once and for all, I tried to tell people what God had done for me. But I found that Christians, especially, are very suspicious and often don't leave room for God to set people free.

I took some hard knocks and disappointments, including losing the camp job, from trying to share what God had helped me through, and I learned to silence my testimony. In fact, I felt God shut my mouth on the topic. For all these years I have kept the lid on what God has done for me and tried to teach and encourage others away from sin without divulging why I so strongly believe my own message. That recent Sunday night, God released me from my fear to claim a background of this nature, and He freed me to be able to speak openly of my past so that He might use it for His glory.

I stood before our congregation and admitted that I had never shared my past with a church before, but that I was not afraid. And I am not afraid to tell you either. My only concern is that you will feel deeply troubled about all of this. If you do, I pray that you will turn that struggle over to our gracious Father in heaven. Thank Him for saving my soul and for a daughter who is sold out to obey Him no matter what He may ask. I assure you that only the Holy Spirit could have gotten me to fearlessly stand and invite people to associate homosexuality with my past. That is a miracle of miracles. But I am free, and I told the church that I would like for them to think I am a wonderful person, but more than that, I want my freedom. Mom and Dad, I have that freedom. I have never felt so good in all of my life. This is a time for praise.

Thank the Lord, this friend received a loving, supportive response from her parents. But not everyone is so gracious. Some people find the past so repugnant that they simply cannot, or will not, look beyond it.

When first faced with a bowl of Raisin Bran, my (Debra's) youngest child, whom my husband and I adopted from Vietnam as a toddler, took one look at the raisins and said, "Bugs!" To this day, she will not eat the raisins in Raisin Bran.

Unfortunately, some of my friend's fellow churchgoers could never look beyond the "bugs" in her past. For years, they had watched her as a leader in their congregation. She teaches. She participates in the music program. She directs special events. She even conducts a Bible study in her community as an independent outreach to others. However, when her home church listened to her testimony, some were inspired and helped, but others condemned her.

She, however, focused upon the One who had delivered her and learned yet another lesson: the freedom of complete dependence upon the Lord. That dependence on Him broke the chains of dependence upon others. Only when Christians are brave enough to truly be transparent can others see the reflection of Christ in them.

> The stoutest armor of defense is that
> which is within the bosom,
> And the weapon that no enemy can parry
> is a bold and cheerful spirit.
>
> **—Anonymous**

# 4
# FINDING THE "YES" IN EVERY MESS

No matter how many promises God has made,
they are "Yes" in Christ.
—2 Cor. 1:20

It all started when I (Debra) decided to put baby oil in my bathwater. I never intended to harm my husband, physically or emotionally. Honest. I simply wanted to pamper myself a bit. So I squeezed a lavish amount of baby oil into my warm bath and lay back to enjoy the moment.

After my "moment" was over, I drained the oversized fiberglass tub, dried off, and started getting ready for bed. My dear unsuspecting husband, Daniel, who is built like a football player, hopped into the tub and closed the shower curtain.

Then the strangest thing began to happen. I say "began to happen" because the event was something that should have occurred in a split second but instead kept *going* and *going* and *going.*

The first thing I heard was a hard thud. Then *a blum-bum-bonk-conk-crash!* Next, some undefined body part, more than likely a hand, elbow, or foot, slammed into the blue shower curtain. It puffed outward like a mushroom.

More thudding. A flop. A few knocks. Another body part assaulted the shower curtain. A roll. A rumble. The sounds of shampoo bottles toppling into the tub. Then—silence.

Poor Daniel, forever the strong, silent sort, never made a noise during the whole ordeal.

Before the initial thud, I was about to brush my teeth. Needless to say, that little chore was postponed. I stood perched in front of the tub, not knowing whether to laugh, cry, or run. I have strong tendencies toward hilarity, so I was naturally on the verge of laughter.

Then I heard dear Daniel attempting to stand. At this point, he still had not uttered one word. He yanked aside the shower curtain and glared at me. Please note that Daniel's eyes are a normal shade of green. However, now they had taken on a strange monster-type glow. The only thing that distracted me from them was the round shiny spot on his reddened cheek, about the size of two silver dollars.

Baby oil, of course.

As the irate stare continued, I forced myself to keep my face impassive, knowing that laughter at this point could be fatal. Finally, Daniel yanked the shower curtain back into place. Still trying to repress the hilarity, I bit my lips until they ached.

Daniel turned on the shower. The warm water must have washed away his fury. I heard a chuckle. A chortle. Then outright laughter. Realizing the "coast was clear," I allowed my own amusement to spew forth.

Only when his shower was over and we were both weakened with laughter did I learn the inside story.

"I just couldn't stop falling!" he exclaimed. "Everything I grabbed was slick! I'd think I was going to stop, and then I'd slide up one side of the tub and back to the other. It was like I was a seal or something!"

Fortunately, the crack in the bathtub was the only lasting injury. Do I even need to tell you I have refrained from baby oil in my bath to this very day?

Humor is the lubricating oil of [life].
It prevents friction and wins good will.

**—Anonymous**

## The Messes of Life

If you have a pulse and are over the age of five, you know there are times when it seems you just can't stop falling. At times, life can be an "oily mess." Nothing goes right, it seems that God has forgotten you, and your world is nothing short of total chaos. You feel as if you've been knocked off your feet and are flopping around in an oily bathtub, trying to grab *anything* to stabilize yourself.

Paul himself experienced such feelings. The local church to whom he said, "No matter how many promises God has made, they are 'Yes' in Christ" (2 Cor. 1:20), was itself in a horrible mess. Factions, fights, and falsehoods were the norm. Paul also had been in a lot of personal messes in his lifetime. Some of them he had caused through his own murderous past. Some occurred to him after his conversion.

In 2 Corinthians, Paul opens his heart to the people in Corinth and tells them about the problems he had encountered. There was opposition to his apostolic authority. Paul had to discipline one of the church members, probably a leader. Furthermore, Paul had to endure a trial so severe that he feared for his life.

And on top of all this, Paul received severe criticism from some of the people in Corinth because he changed his plan and apparently had not kept his promise. He promised to visit the Corinthians not once, but twice—once on the way to Macedonia and again on the way back.

However, he had to change his plans. Plan A failed, and Plan B was a wash. He was harshly criticized. His critics said if Paul says one thing, he really means another. His *yes* is *no* and his *no* is *yes*. This prompted the apostle to write about *God's "Yes" in every mess.*

## The "Yes" in the Mess

There is a "Yes" in every failure and tragedy. In his letter to Roman Christians, Paul restates the principle, "We know that in all things God works for the good of those who love him, who have been called according to his purpose" (Rom. 8:28).

We've often heard the question "Why do bad things happen to good people?" It presupposes that good people should be exempt from tragedy, should receive a "get out of jail free" card, should be hermetically sealed and excluded from tragedy. But the truth is that bad things happen to *all* people. *Everyone* encounters tragedies. We *all* fail at times.

## The Causes

Tragedies have various causes. Some are caused by the disobedience of people. For example, people break laws—both moral and civic—and the results are tragic, like those of the 1995 Oklahoma City bombing. Other tragedies have natural causes, like the devastating tornado that struck the same city only a few years later.

But for the Christian there is no such thing as a "senseless tragedy." Every incident in the Christian's life has a God-planned purpose—"in all things God works for the good." Does that suggest that God causes or allows them out of some spite for His creation? Certainly not.

And does that guarantee that tragedies will make any sense to us? Of course not. It does mean, however, that there is no tragedy that cannot eventually be used for positive purpose. There's a "Yes" in every mess.

In bad career choices.

In a difficult marriage.

In financial reverses.

In the loss of good health.

The "Yes" is Jesus Christ.

Paul himself demonstrates the radical power of this "Yes." He is a clear example of a man who was a mess-maker. Consider who he was before his Acts 9 encounter with Jesus Christ. He certainly had chosen a bad career. Making a life of killing Christians isn't exactly a high and holy calling.

Saying that he was separated from the will of God would be an understatement. Yet despite his disobedience to God, he had a spiritual encounter with the Lord of the universe. And that encounter bumped him into a new realm of existence, into a new career, into a new discovery of God's perfect will.

## None of Us Are Exempt

Paul also exemplifies that an experience with Christ does not exempt us from the messes of life. Even after his Damascus road encounter with God, Paul had his difficulties—difficulties in his relationships with other Christians, and physical difficulties, including his own "thorn in [the] flesh" (2 Cor. 12:7). Also, his various imprisonments brought him financial reverses.

Nevertheless, he wrote, "The Son of God, Jesus Christ, who was preached among you by me and Silas and Timothy, was not 'Yes' and 'No,' but in him it has always been 'Yes.' For no matter how many promises God has made, they are 'Yes' in Christ. And so through him the 'Amen' is spoken by us to the glory of God. Now it is God who makes both us and you stand firm in Christ. He anointed us, set his seal of ownership on us, and put his Spirit in our hearts as a deposit, guaranteeing what is to come" (2 Cor. 1:19-22).

Truly Jesus Christ is the "Yes" in every mess!
If He is not the "Yes,"
If He can't be the "Yes,"
If He won't be the "Yes,"
Then we must write "No"
Across every reality of life.

—Stan Toler

## The Mess at Wedgwood Baptist Church

Most of us know about the tragedy at Wedgwood Baptist Church in Fort Worth, Texas, when a gunman walked into a church service and killed seven people. I (Debra) was truly grieved when I came home from church that Wednesday night, September 15, 1999, and saw the news report of what had happened not so far from my home in east Texas. All I could think is, "What are we coming to?"

The next morning during my prayer time, I cried out to God on behalf of those families whose loved ones had died, as well as for the church as a whole. I had gotten only a few minutes into my prayer when the Lord strongly impressed upon me that this tragedy had been allowed to further His gospel and His kingdom. An unspeakable peace fell over me. Even though I didn't understand all the implications of what the Lord had spoken to me, I knew He was in control.

A few weeks later I began to hear the details of the awesome way in which God was using the loss of those seven individuals, each of whom were strong Christians.

> You intended to harm me, but God intended it
> for good to accomplish what is now being done,
> the saving of many lives.
> —Gen. 50:20

The *Baptist Standard* reported that a United Methodist church in Fort Worth sent 15 people to Wedgwood on the Sunday after the shooting to cover the church's child care needs so that no adults would have to miss the service.

Members of a church in Tulsa, Oklahoma, drove five hours so they could march around Wedgwood Church and pray during its services that Sunday.

One of the youth who was wounded protecting her friend has scoliosis. The curve in her spine may have allowed the bullet to miss major organs as it passed through her, saving her from serious injury.

A number of teenagers have professed faith in Jesus Christ at Fort Worth schools and throughout Tarrant County since the shooting.

Wedgwood has received strong support from Christians around the world. As of October 6, 1999, just three weeks since the tragedy, the church had received more than 13,000 E-mails, 20,000 cards and letters, hundreds of posters and banners, and $100,000 in donations. Those E-mails, cards, letters, posters, and banners now line the hallways of the church.

Wedgwood Pastor Al Meredith led a call to prayer. "What has emerged from the tragic shooting in our church on September 15 is a clear message of hope and faith in our God, even in the darkest hours," Meredith said. He called his church to 40 days of concerted prayer "for spiritual awakening in our nation."

"The Wedgwood tragedy also has energized the prayer lives of many members of First Baptist Church of White Settlement and other churches in Tarrant County," added Jim Gatliff, pastor of the suburban Fort Worth church. One of the youths killed at Wedgwood, Joey Ennis, was from his church's youth group, and another member of the White Settlement youth group was seriously wounded.

"Probably the biggest difference I have seen is in prayer," Gatliff added. "We have Christians all over this city who are praying for revival."

Some think revival already may have begun. Forty-two students at a school near Wedgwood recently professed faith in Christ, and the White Settlement church pastor said more than 100 have become Christians through the rallies and the funeral of Joey Ennis.

He went on to say that many of those making commitments already are beginning to attend area churches. There also has been a rise in the commitment level among Wedgwood members who made decisions for Christ before the shooting. He commented, "The number one thing I've noticed is a renewed commitment to the Body of Christ. We are seeing people back in church whom we haven't seen for a very long time."

Christians also are demonstrating a greater commitment to one another, the pastor added. "We linger longer with one another. Worship services end, but the people don't leave. They stay and talk with one another. I hear a lot more people telling one another, 'I love you.' I see a lot more people hugging."[1]

God has clearly demonstrated, and continues to demonstrate, His awesome power, love, and sovereignty even in the midst of this catastrophe. I am convinced that there will be even more mighty works over which to rejoice.

Truly, He is our "Yes" in every mess of life!

> I thank my God through Jesus Christ for all of you,
> because your faith is being reported
> all over the world.
>
> —Rom. 1:8

> Circumstances are like a feather bed—
> comfortable if you're on top,
> but smothering if you're underneath.
>
> —Anonymous

### The Doughnut Shop

In Oklahoma City, where I (Stan) pastor, we have a chain of doughnut stores called Daylight Donuts—the best in the Southwest! I love their doughnuts—and it shows. I think everybody else in Oklahoma City likes their doughnuts too. In fact, parking places are scarce at their stores in the morning.

One Monday morning I found myself in spiritual warfare. Do I stay true to my diet, or do I go to the doughnut shop for a blueberry, cream-filled doughnut and a Diet Coke?

Well, I began to pray, *Lord, you know how busy Daylight Donuts is this time of day. If you want me to have a doughnut, you'll just have to make a parking spot available right in front of the store.*

Don't you know, after my *seventh* time around the block, a spot miraculously opened up right in front of the door! Don't tell *me* seven isn't God's perfect number!

## God's People Buried Under a Mess

In 2 Chron. 20, God's people were buried under a mess and needed a greater miracle than a parking place. Three different groups of enemies were attacking them. Three-to-one odds!

Ever had a day when you felt as if everybody were against you? That's how the children of Israel felt.

The first thing Jehoshaphat did was fast and seek God's help. That's a good place to start when you need a miracle in the mess.

Then he began recalling the many times God had provided for them before. That gave him a *faith lift!*

In verses 9 and 20, King Jehoshaphat admitted to God that he was absolutely powerless. (That's when God works miracles—when we admit that it won't happen without God's power.)

I like what Jehoshaphat did next. He told his army to start singing praises to the Lord.

What happened next is either miraculous—or those boys were bad singers! The three groups of Israel's enemies destroyed *one another.*

What a God! He is the God of miracles—and parking places in front of doughnut shops.

## Steps to Overcoming the Mess

Perhaps you're so overwhelmed by life's circumstances that you just want out. Perhaps you think, "Maybe Jesus is the 'Yes,' but how does that help me survive *this* mess?" We often have no control over the circumstances life delivers, but like Jehoshaphat, we can make some choices that will empower us to live above them.

Here's what you can do to start finding the "Yes" in every mess:

**First, focus on God.** "Blessed are they who keep his statutes and seek him with all their heart" (Ps. 119:2). We hear a lot about "focus." It's everywhere, from athletic events to aerobics classes. Focusing means centering your attention and ignoring the things around you. Focusing on God means centering your attention on Him, not the surrounding circumstances. Spend some top-quality time with the Lord. Read His Word. Talk to Him about the mess you're in. Confess your faith in His ability to make a "Yes" out of it.

**Second, begin a fast.** "This kind does not go out except by prayer and fasting" (Matt. 17:21, NKJV). That was Jesus' answer to the disciples when they weren't able to cast out a demon from a young boy.

"Fasting" means doing without an essential or nonessential, such as television viewing, food, and so on, in order to spend that time in prayer. Such self-denial intensifies your desires for deliverance and speaks your determination to God.

**Third, praise God for His continuing faithfulness.** David wrote, "I will sing of the LORD's great love forever; with my mouth I will make your faithfulness known through all generations. I will declare that your love stands firm forever, that you established your faithfulness in heaven itself" (Ps. 89:1-2).

Do you remember past messes? Do you remember how God saw you through them. You trusted Him then. You can trust Him now. His faithfulness has not changed.

**Fourth, declare your faith in God's power.** "I will sing of Your power; yes, I will sing aloud of Your mercy in the morning; for You have been my defense and refuge in the day of my trouble" (Ps. 59:16, NKJV).

When life gets a little messy, you can be sure that God is a fortress, a place where you can flee. That place of refuge is surrounded by His might. His infinite power can extinguish the fiery arrows of doubt and the destructive forces of hell itself. Declare His power. Reaffirm your faith in His ability to protect you, even in the mess.

**Fifth, consider His way the best.** "I will proclaim the name of the LORD. Oh, praise the greatness of our God! He is the Rock, his works are perfect, and all his ways are just. A faithful God who does no wrong, upright and just is he" (Deut. 32:3-4).

True praise occurs only when independent of pleasant circumstances. Praising God when the sun shines is easy. Praising Him when the storm clouds start moving in and we can't see the way proves more challenging. But praise is an act of willful trust in His infinite wisdom and deliverance. In fact, praise brings peace to our spirits.

> *There is peace in the midst of my storm-tossed life;*
> *Oh, there's an Anchor, there's a Rock to cast my faith upon.*
> *Jesus rides in my vessel, so I'll fear no alarm;*
> *He gives me peace in the midst of my storm!**
>
> —Stephen R. Adams

## Finding the "Yes" in the Tornado

Finding the "Yes" in a slight thunderstorm is one thing, but finding it in a terrifying tornado is quite another. My (Debra's) husband, Daniel, and I recently took the children to Six Flags over Texas in Arlington. A lightning storm began gathering, which resulted in the rides closing, so we decided to go home early. As we were driving from the park, a monstrous, funnel-shaped cloud formed on the edge of the line of dark clouds.

I don't have many fears in life—only snakes, dark alleys where strange men lurk, and *tornadoes.* In east Texas tornadoes are a way of life in the spring and autumn. But no matter how many times I endure a tornado warning or watch, I never get used to them.

"That's a tornado! I know it's a tornado! It's got to be a tornado!" I said, quieting my voice from the screams I wanted to erupt into a mild form of yelling.

---

"That's not a tornado," my husband—the strong, silent sort—calmly insisted. "The policeman we asked said the National Weather Service declared that it *isn't* a tornado!"

"I don't care what the National Weather Service or what the policeman says—it's a tornado!" I insisted, my stomach churning as I watched the dark funnel cloud take on an elegant tail that formed itself into a graceful hook at the end. "I know a tornado when I see one!"

"It's *not* a tornado."

"Well, if that isn't a tornado, then it's got to be a funnel cloud. What exactly is the definition of a funnel cloud anyway? Is it just a funnel-shaped cloud?"

"I don't know."

"Well, I think that could clearly be defined as a funnel cloud," I said, pointing toward the black monster.

"It isn't a tornado. You're going to scare the kids to death."

"Well, *I'm* scared to death." Little did Daniel know that he and the children were getting an extremely calm version of the hair-pulling, shrieking, terrified wails forming in my soul.

I vocalized a few prayers.

"What?" Daniel asked.

"I'm praying!"

And I continued to pray. Only minutes after we had driven from the influence of that intimidating funnel cloud we were accosted by a severe storm that turned the sky and road into one gray entity. The wind shoved against the van. Hail spattered us. We joined the other cars creeping forward in traffic. And soon all the vehicles stopped along the side of the road.

Immediately I recalled the tornado I had driven through five years before. I never saw the funnel, but I did hear the warning over the radio to take cover, and I did drive through rain, wind, and hail, which almost matched what we were experiencing.

"I've been here before," I muttered, still terrified.

Daniel had now taken on a grim expression that spoke of his equal concern. I decided to pull down the blinds in the van, hoping to protect the children if the glass should shatter. I noticed one driver who had driven his vehicle across the ditch, as if he expected to be blown away at any moment. Apparently, he was as anxious as we were.

But at long last the storm began subsiding, and we were able to creep back into traffic. Later I learned that Daniel, the policeman, *and* the National Weather Service were right. That funnel cloud really wasn't a tornado; it just looked like one—so much so that the television weatherman put it on the local nightly news with claims that it *could have* developed into a tornado. I thank God that we were spared during that storm.

Though that storm missed us, many tornadoes have struck others in countless locations through the years, leaving a wake of destruction.

I (Stan) saw such a "tornado" with my family when my father was killed in the construction accident. My mother discovered that Jesus was indeed her "Yes" in the mess of her life.

Three months before Aaron Toler's electrocution, my mother, Loretta Toler (now Hollingsworth), almost died herself. At the age of 30, she underwent major surgery and lost a substantial amount of blood. She awoke in the hospital, drenched in sweat, certain that this was the end. So sure was she of her death that she asked the nurse to please call her husband and her minister. Mom survived, only to learn later that she had gone into shock and desperately needed a blood transfusion, which she never received.

Due to complications from the surgery, Mom developed a hormonal imbalance, which required her to go to the doctor and take injections every day. This condition left her highly nervous, to the point of not even being able to tolerate someone walking up the stairway. It was an entire month before she was back on her feet.

## Day of Recovery, Day of Death

August 31, 1962, the very day my mother began seeing signs of recovery, was the day her husband died by electrocution in a construction accident. On that day she had driven us three boys to a mall to buy school clothes for the oldest of us, Terry and me. When she arrived home from the mall that afternoon, her brother met her, saying the police had been looking for her.

He hedged about the seriousness of my father's condition. Even when she discovered that Dad had been electrocuted, my mother never felt that he would really die.

Soon after arriving at the hospital, she learned the details. As a construction worker, Dad had been operating a crane atop the new pharmacy under construction across the street from the hospital. Amid the drizzle, he had two hands on a metal wire that touched a live electrical wire. His fellow worker had only one hand on the wire, and his life was spared.

While rushing to the intensive care unit (ICU) where Dad lay dying, Mom reflected on the irony of moving from West Virginia to Columbus, Ohio. Dad had accepted a job as a construction worker, one that promised us a much better life, well above the poverty level of a coal miner's life. And since he was already struggling with black lung disease, he desperately needed to get out of the mines, simply to survive. How awful that the move, intended to extend his life and improve conditions for his family, resulted in this tragedy—this "tornado"!

At last Mom stood beside her husband in the ICU, where he lay unconscious. With her pastor and his wife on one side of the bed and her on the other, she relived the past: the day she met Aaron Toler; the first time she realized she loved him; the day of their simple wedding; Aaron's exultation when she told him she was going to have a child; the miraculous birth of her first son, Stan, in spite of the doctor's prediction that she would never have children; the equal exultation Dad displayed when God blessed them with two more boys.

As the past engulfed her thoughts, Mom begged her husband to live. "I love you, Aaron. You know how much I love you. You can't leave us," she pleaded. "You have to stay with us. We have three little boys we have to raise. Please, please, Aaron."

As he lay on his deathbed, tears like rivulets of sorrow began streaming down his cheeks. Mom knew beyond doubt that the man who had been her friend, her lover, her spouse had indeed heard her. The doctors claimed he could not hear, that he was so firmly in the grips of unconsciousness that he understood nothing. But Mom knew differently.

## Peace in the Eye of the Storm

After visiting with Dad, Mom went to the hospital chapel with her pastor and his wife at her side. The chapel was the same as that in many other hospitals: a small, shadowed room with stained-glass windows. A cross. An altar. A few pews. As Mom knelt to beseech the Lord, an indescribable calm settled into her soul, a peace that she interpreted as heavenly assurance that her husband would certainly *live.*

With Mom praying and believing that Dad would indeed live, he survived a miraculous six hours following the accident—which astounded the doctors. Soon Dad went to be with the Lord whom he loved. The doctors wanted to do an autopsy to discover the reason he lasted so long despite his grave condition. Mom refused and told them she fully understood the reason he lingered with them: He wanted to live. He had a wonderful family. He didn't want to die. He needed to continue as a husband and father and devout church member.

## More Storm Clouds

After Dad's death, Mom began a journey into depression. Because of her continued problems with hormonal imbalance, her depression was accompanied by the severe nervousness that had plagued her even before Dad's death. But she knew that somehow she had to be strong for her grieving boys. Now, Mom says, "I know God gave me the best children in the world, or I would have never made it. In all honesty, I feel like I was to blame for Stan growing up too soon. I told him he had to be the 'little man' of the house now, and I feel as if perhaps I robbed him of his childhood."

Our lives had been thrown into a mess—a full-blown "torna-do," and through her depression Mom dealt with the whole ordeal the best she could.

## "Where Is God?"

As she sank lower and lower into what felt like a black abyss, Mom began "talking" to her deceased husband more and more. She felt as if God was nowhere to be found; it seemed that He didn't even hear her prayers. She spent hours in prayer, crying out to God, only to feel all the more empty and hopeless. At last, at her darkest moment, she felt she could pray no longer, so she asked her depart-ed husband to "go to God for her and beg His intervention."

She says, "I know that makes no sense, but that's just how low I was. Finally, I could bear it no more. I prayed so long and so hard that I believe the Lord gave me a vision of Aaron. He was standing in the bedroom doorway, and I felt that he was telling me every-thing would be all right. I don't believe I actually *saw* Aaron, but I think the Lord, in His mercy and love, gave me a vision of him to comfort me."

## Discovering the "Yes" in the Tornado

That moment was the turning point for my mother. That's when she knew that Jesus was the "Yes" in her mess. She had dis-covered His triumph in the "tornado" of her life.

God had already been at work. First, Dad had taken out a small life insurance policy only months before his death. Given the insur-ance, plus the Social Security payments for us boys, and the settle-ment she received from the state at Dad's death, Mom was not thrown into poverty or forced to go to work. Second, even though Dad died young, Mom took comfort in knowing he would never have to suffer the horrible prolonged death associated with his black lung condition. Third, God began a work in the heart of a single young man who attended our church.

Jack Hollingsworth, three years Mom's junior, had never married. Before Dad's death, Jack and our family had known each other at a distance. But Jack was so moved by Dad's death that he testified at his home church in Kentucky that he couldn't understand why the Lord would allow the death of such a wonderful man of God who had three boys to raise. He claimed that he wished the Lord had taken him instead of my dad.

Even though Mom had no plans to ever get married again, a few months later, she and Jack began dating. Eventually, they fell in love—and one year after Dad's death, they married. God provided a wonderful stepfather for Terry and Mark and me. He also gave our mom a second chance at love. Certainly, God's grace was evident to all.

"God served as my psychiatrist," Mom claims. And as He does for all of us, He proved a faithful friend, deliverer, and healer.

> Whether we are mess makers or mess takers,
> Jesus is ready to be our "Yes!"
>
> —Debra White Smith

## Finding the "Yes" in the Oklahoma City Tornado

On May 3, 1999, the Thurman family took shelter in a closet of their new home on Shorehan Court in Oklahoma City. Randy, Pati, and three-year-old Levi covered themselves with a blanket as a force-5 tornado passed by. In a matter of seconds their house was gone. Only the three-square-foot piece of carpet on which they stood remained.

Finding the "Yes" in that mess has been easy for the Thurmans. They survived unharmed and were able to build a new home to replace the old. (They even framed the piece of carpet as a testimony to God's faithfulness.) Here are some positive things that Randy testifies can happen when you live through a tornado or any other tragedy:

- You understand that God is fully in control. God is Lord over the storms of life.

- You appreciate the therapeutic value of humor. Proverbs tells us, "A merry heart does good, like medicine" (17:22, NKJV). That was evident to Randy after the tornado. He was able to laugh in spite of his loss when he saw a chewed-up pickup truck bearing a sign reading, "Don't scratch my paint."

- You understand that real wealth is not dependent on your real estate holdings, but rather in the relationship you have with your God and your family.

- You are humbled and learn how to be a receiver. Randy and his family discovered real community in the help they received from others.

- You learn to pay attention to the details. Randy discovered the importance of having the right property insurance and reading the fine print in the policy.

- The clutter is eliminated. Spring cleaning would never be easier!

- Your friends and family show how much they care.

- You are provided an easy way to share God's miracles and grace with others.

- You focus not on trying to figure God out, but rather on getting to *know* Him.

- You stop putting on false fronts, like putting Aunt Ruth's purple rug out before she comes over.

- The "honey do" list is drastically reduced. (Suddenly the attic clutter wasn't a problem.)

Randy found a humor in the horror. And so can you. If you're living in a mess and can't find the "Yes," keep looking. Develop an unshakable belief in God's providential care.

Persist.

Persevere.

Don't throw in the towel.

Look for the opportunity that adversity always presents. Visit with others who have suffered setbacks. And get on with life! All of God's promises are "Yes" in Christ!

A cheerful heart is good medicine.

—Prov. 17:22

# 5
# "HELP! I'M SINKING!"
## DEALING WITH FAILURE

Peter got down out of the boat, walked on the
water and came toward Jesus. But when he saw
the wind, he was afraid and, beginning to sink,
cried out, "Lord, save me!"
—Matt. 14:29-30

I (Debra) have a friend, Nancy Scruggs, who tells a humorous story of three women in rural east Texas who went shopping in a nearby town. They spent an enjoyable evening and embarked on their journey homeward. They hadn't been on the highway long when they noticed a dead cat lying near the shoulder of the road. Being notorious cat lovers, they decided to stop and pick up the poor creature, take him home, and give him a proper burial.

Now they were faced with the dilemma of what to wrap the cat in. Certainly they didn't want to just flop his carcass onto the floorboard. After some thinking, one of them decided to empty her purchases from an elegant department store bag and use the bag as a transitional casket.

With the expired feline resting in the department store "casket" on the back floor, the trio resumed their journey.

Passing a fast-food restaurant, they were reminded how long it had been since they had eaten and decided to stop. After considering the condition of their dead passenger, they chose to place the bagged cat outside the car while they ate inside. They simply didn't feel comfortable leaving him shut up in the car. He didn't smell like daisies, and the car would be airtight on a hot Texas night. So they propped the "casket" against a tire and entered the restaurant to enjoy their meal.

Not long after they were seated and eating, an elderly woman entered the restaurant carrying a department store bag that was strangely familiar.

The trio exchanged concerned glances and then looked out the large window.

Yes, the bagged cat was gone.

The poor woman holding the bag must have thought she had retrieved some valuable find that someone had accidentally left. As the lady stood in line to place her order, she decided to glance into the bag for the first time.

Bad move for a heart patient! She immediately dropped the bag and gripped her chest. Soon surrounding customers noticed her distress and alerted the manager, who promptly called an ambulance. Since the hospital was only a block away, the ambulance arrived quickly, and within minutes the elderly lady was loaded into the emergency vehicle.

The conscientious paramedics, making sure they included *all* the lady's belongings, threw the bagged cat in the ambulance near the gurney.

That was the last those cat-loving shoppers saw of their feline friend.

## Spiraling Out of Control

How often we get ourselves into circumstances that quickly spiral out of control. And often those circumstances had a noble beginning. We intend a deed to be honorable or humane and inadvertently we cause someone else to have a "heart attack."

Sometimes these "heart attacks" take the form of broken relationships, heated words, unwise choices, fears, failures, desperation, and heartache. But the greatest thing in life is to discover, or rediscover, a God who wants to take our hand and walk us through those out-of-control circumstances.

He did just that for the apostle named Peter.

> Lying in bed with Snoopy, Charlie Brown said,
> "Sometimes I lie awake at night and ask,
> 'Where have I gone wrong?' Then a voice says to me,
> 'This is going to take more than one night!'"

## The Sinkers Among Us

Jesus and His disciples had experienced a busy day of ministry. They were tired and ready for some time alone. The Gospel writer describes what happened next:

Jesus made the disciples get into the boat and go on ahead of him to the other side, while he dismissed the crowd. After he had dismissed them, he went up on a mountainside by himself to pray. When evening came, he was there alone, but the boat was already a considerable distance from land, buffeted by the waves because the wind was against it.

During the fourth watch of the night Jesus went out to them, walking on the lake. When the disciples saw him walking on the lake, they were terrified. "It's a ghost," they said, and cried out in fear.

But Jesus immediately said to them: "Take courage! It is I. Don't be afraid."

"Lord, if it's you," Peter replied, "tell me to come to you on the water."

"Come," he said.

Then Peter got down out of the boat, walked on the water and came toward Jesus. But when he saw the wind, he was afraid and, beginning to sink, cried out, "Lord, save me!"

Immediately Jesus reached out his hand and caught him. "You of little faith," he said, "why did you doubt?"

And when they climbed into the boat, the wind died down. Then those who were in the boat worshipped him, saying, "Truly you are the Son of God" *(Matt. 14:22-33).*

Unlike our modern, recreational perceptions of the sea, in the ancient world the sea was seen as something to be feared. Some cultures even believed the sea was the setting for conflict between the gods. Stephen J. Lennox writes of some those fears:

Mesopotamia dreaded the sea monster, Tiamat. Canaanite culture feared Yam, challenger of the creator god, Baal. They also spoke of Lotan, a sea monster that Baal defeated. Some believe that Lotan may be the creature the Bible refers to as Leviathan (Job 3:8; 41:1; Psalm 74:14; 104:26; Isaiah 27:1), over whom God exercises complete control.[1]

## Our Stormy Seas

We may not have such fears of the ocean rooted in ancient mythology, but we do have our own fears. Imagine that this tempestuous sea onto which Peter stepped represented something that we fear. Imagine that those billowing waves represent some circumstance that's swallowing us up.

We may even have our own "sea monsters" lurking beneath the surface of our lives. And, like Peter, this "sea" may be something we have jumped into ourselves. Or, it might even be an expanse that God directed us to sail across, in some "heavenly assignment." Notice that the disciples were in this storm between 3 and 6 A.M. because Jesus *told* them to go out to sea a few hours earlier.

Getting caught in the storm was a direct result of their obedience to the Lord! And while the apostle's bailing out of the boat and onto the stormy seas was initially his idea, he jumped out only after Jesus Christ said, "Come."

## The Lord of the Waves

The circumstances in which we are sinking may be the result of some step that God has ordained, or they may be the result of a personal choice (or the choice someone asked us to make). It may even be the result of some situation out of our control. But the beauty of the story is this: Jesus is Lord of the waves!

Again, Lennox writes:

> When Jesus stepped from the shore and began His walk on the surface of the Sea of Galilee, He was not just taking a convenient shortcut. He wanted to do more than just impress the disciples with His miraculous power. Jesus' journey on the stormy waters was a demonstration of God's control over chaos. Broil and foam as it may, the sea became solid as stone beneath His sandals. And once again, His power stilled the storm to a whisper.[2]

The Sea of Galilee itself may be a metaphor for life's often-difficult journey. According to Robert Q. Bailey, "The Sea of Galilee is a freshwater lake, approximately 13 miles long and 8 miles wide. Its elevation (700 feet below sea level) contrasts to surrounding Mount Hermon (over 9,200 feet high). The east-west ridges of Galilee form 'wind tunnels' that help create the sudden and violent storms for which the area is famous."[3]

## Unexpected Winds

The disciples were trying to cross only eight miles of water and ended up rowing all night because of unexpected winds.

How often in life have we felt as if we were rowing all night against contrary winds? And how often have our circumstances loomed over us just as Mount Hermon dwarfed the disciples on the Sea of Galilee?

We know that the storms can appear to build moment by moment. There we are, rowing against the storms! No wonder we sometimes get our eyes off the One who walks the waves.

Obviously Peter was a sinker. Like many of us, his step-out-of-the-boat faith dwindled fast and left him a sudden victim of his surroundings. When he forgot his source of power, he began to doubt. Doubt bred fear. And soon, he sank.

## A Saving Sequence

Peter's lack of "sea legs" demonstrates the cycle of fear that some of us have been caught in at one time or another. Look at the sequence in the Scripture. When he saw the wind, Peter came face-to-face with *reality*. When he cried out, Peter *reacted* to the situation. When he began to sink, Peter faced the *consequences* of his fear. When he called, "Lord, save me!" Peter exercised renewed *faith*.

Faith breaks the cycle of fear. Without faith we will experience a never-ending circle of fear. Consequences will stack up like the mountain ridges around Galilee. And we just go on to the next storm. We become professional dog-paddlers in the seas of despair. Soon our emotional muscles will tire. And eventually we will be so overcome by life's heartaches that we feel as if we're drowning, as if there's no spiritual life left within our souls. But, thank God, there's a Rock to stand on, no matter how stormy or how deep the sea!

> *My hope is built on nothing less*
> *Than Jesus' blood and righteousness.*
> *I dare not trust the sweetest frame,*
> *But wholly lean on Jesus' name.*
>
> *When darkness seems to hide His face,*
> *I rest on His unchanging grace.*
> *In ev'ry high and stormy gale,*
> *My anchor holds within the veil.*
>
> *His oath, His covenant, His blood,*
> *Support me in the whelming flood.*
> *When all around my soul gives way,*
> *He then is all my Hope and Stay.*
>
> *When He shall come with trumpet sound,*
> *O may I then in Him be found!*
> *Dressed in His righteousness alone,*
> *Faultless to stand before the throne!*

*On Christ, the solid Rock, I stand;*
*All other ground is sinking sand.*
*All other ground is sinking sand.*

—Edward Mote

## Is a Sinker a Failure?

Jonas Salk had his sinking moments. He developed 200 unsuccessful vaccines for polio before he came up with one that worked. Someone asked him, "How did it feel to fail 200 times trying to invent a vaccine for polio?"

He responded, "I never failed 200 times at anything in my life. My family taught me never to use that word. I simply discovered 200 ways how *not* to make a vaccine for polio."

Winston Churchill had his sinking moments. Someone asked that great statesman, "What most prepared you to lead Great Britain through World War II?" For a period of time, Great Britain had stood virtually alone against Nazi Germany as it dominated the Western world.

Churchill said, "It was the time I repeated a class in grade school."

"You mean you flunked a grade?"

"I never flunked in my life," Churchill reasoned. "I was given a second opportunity to get it right."

Sinkers aren't necessarily failures.

We never test the resources of God
until we attempt the impossible.

—Stan Toler

When we read the story of the sinking disciple, it's easy to think of him as a failure. He did fail in the sense that he lost focus on Jesus and allowed fear to engulf him.

But don't forget—Peter was the only disciple in that creaking, waterlogged, rocking boat that had enough initial faith to actually step from the safety of the boat to the uncertainty of the sea.

While Peter was doing the backstroke, 11 bigger failures sat in the boat. They failed privately. They failed quietly. Their failure was safe, unnoticed, and uncriticized. Only Peter experienced the *public* "failure."

However, only Peter experienced the glory of walking on the water. He was the only passenger in that vessel who understood the depths of Jesus' ability to save people who are sinking in the seas of their circumstances.

Like Peter, we've had those "sinking feelings." We've focused on the seas instead of the Savior. We've taken dynamic steps and ended up in the drink. But we're not failures until we refuse to call out to Christ in faith, until we refuse to extend our hand to Him, until we decide not to allow Him to lift us above our stormy situation.

## Reckless Faith All-Stars

Truly He is the God of the elements, the God of our fears, the God of our faith. He is worthy of our reckless faith. Notice some of these "reckless faith" all-stars in the Scriptures:

- The woman with the lingering illness who touched the hem of Jesus' garment
- The men who cut a hole through the roof and let a sick man down to be healed by the Great Physician
- Elisha, who floated an axhead in the water
- Naaman, the "7-up saint," who dipped in the water seven times and was cured of leprosy
- Jacob, who wrestled an angel
- Moses' mother, who set Moses afloat in the bulrushes
- Moses himself, who saw the burning bush and dared to say to Jehovah, "Could we talk?"

But none of them walked on the water. Only Peter the "failure" walked on the water!

The apostle heard the voice of his Master above the noise of the tossing waves. "It is I, " Jesus announced to the disciples as He walked on the waves toward them. That phrase is translated, "I am." Peter didn't have much time for a Bible study, but the experience proved to him that the "It is I" of the storm-tossed ocean was the same great "I am" of Moses' burning bush. Jesus himself announced His eternal deity: "'I tell you the truth,' Jesus answered, 'before Abraham was born, I am!'" (John 8:58).

## The Alpha and Omega

John the Revelator caught a vision of His greatness as he, too, heard His voice, saying, "I am the Alpha and the Omega, the Beginning and the End. To him who is thirsty I will give to drink without cost from the spring of the water of life. He who overcomes will inherit all this, and I will be his God and he will be my son" (Rev. 21:6-8).

We never test the resources of God until we attempt the impossible. Sinkers are not failures. They are the ones who have enough faith to get out of the boat!

### Wave Walkers

*Many of us are "wannabes."*
*We would like to be wave walkers.*
*We'd love to get out of the boat.*
*But the boat is safe.*
*The boat is secure.*
*And the boat is comfortable.*
*The water is high.*
*The waves are rough.*
*The wind is strong.*
*And the night is dark.*
*A storm is out there,*
*And if we get out of the boat,*
*We might sink.*
*But if we stay in the boat,*
*We will never walk the waves.*[4]
—Terry Toler

## Faith Steps for the Sinking

An old pilot's adage goes like this: "I'd rather be down here wanting to be up there than to be up there wanting to be down here."

Those words came alive for me (Stan) several years ago when a businessman in my church invited me on a quick flight to Columbus, Ohio. He enlisted a man in our congregation to pilot the plane. I was as trusting as a new baby. I didn't ask any questions about the credentials of the pilot or the condition of the airplane.

It wasn't until we were airborne that the subject of flying into a busy, controlled airport after dark came up. It was then that Jim, the pilot, revealed that it was something he had never done before but had always wanted to do.

That's when I got the first lump in my throat. It also marked the beginning of one fervent, high-altitude prayer meeting.

Every time Jim would fumble with the radio, the map, or even scratch his head, in my mind I would increase my church building pledge and volunteer for missionary service. There was a crisis of trust going on in that little airplane: I did not trust that pilot!

I recently received some E-mail humor about an airline that had a mix-up in its schedule. The passengers waited for several minutes in confusion concerning the destination of the flight. The plane didn't move away from the gate, and the crew seemed to be deep in discussion.

Finally a flight attendant made an announcement. "There seems to be some confusion about the destination of this flight. If your destination is Omaha, please remain seated. If your destination is Dallas, you are asked to exit the plane at this time."

Suddenly the door to the cockpit opened, and the pilot put on his coat, grabbed his flight case, tipped his hat to the passengers, and said, "Sorry, folks—I've got the wrong plane."

Can you imagine the sinking feeling the passengers going to Dallas had? In a larger sense, some people face such feelings every day. They wake up wondering, *Who's in control, and do they know where they're going?*

If you've had some questions like that, here are some steps I would advise you to take:

**Seek God's deliverance above human deliverance.** "You are my help and my deliverer; O my God, do not delay" (Ps. 40:17). Some folks work their way through the entire yellow pages section of the phone book before they get to God. They seek everything from aspirin to acupuncture to deal with their dilemmas—when deliverance is only a prayer away. Superhuman situations need supernatural intervention.

Peter was in a situation that the Coast Guard couldn't help. He needed a Savior—and Jesus was there. He is always ready to reach for us and safely put us back in the boat before we go under.

**Believe God in spite of the storm.** "God has not given us a spirit of fear, but of power and of love and of a sound mind" (2 Tim. 1:7, NKJV). Three hundred sixty-five times in Scripture we are told, "Fear not." That assurance is built on the foundation of God's character, not our crisis. Even when you can't see the Pilot of your soul, you can be assured that He is firmly in control—and He knows where He is going.

**Focus on the things you can change, and forget the rest.** The psalmist is surrounded by turmoil, but he makes a decision of faith: "God is our refuge and strength, an ever-present help in trouble. Therefore we will not fear, though the earth give way and the mountains fall into the heart of the sea, though its waters roar and foam and the mountains quake with their surging" (Ps. 46:1-3).

He knew he probably couldn't change his *altitude,* but he *could* change his *attitude.* He couldn't change the threats, but he *could* change his trust—he decided to praise the God who was a refuge, strength, and help in trouble.

Humor is the lifeboat we use on life's river.

—Anonymous

## Getting into the Boat

A funny thing happened once when my husband and I (Debra) took our son, Brett, fishing in our boat. That boat had "real character." A beautiful shade of faded lime green, it looked as if it dated back to the days of Noah.

There we sat in our watercraft when a truly splendid emerald-colored ski boat appeared behind us. At the back of it, behind the seats, a large, flat area provided enough space for an adult to lie down in the sun.

In this boat sat about six to eight young women, appearing to be in their early 20s. If they had pieced together all the material from their scanty bikinis, I doubt that one modest swimsuit could have been formed. All but one of the girls sat in the front of the boat, either in seats or on the edge, near the driver's seat. The other one was lying facedown on the back part of the boat.

So there they were—cruising behind our family. Three-year-old Brett sharply turned his little head and began intently peering over his shoulder toward the passengers. As they trolled directly behind us, Brett turned and continued his scrutiny over his shoulder. I could almost see his mind whirling with the implications of this sight before him. I said nothing, just waiting for him to voice his thoughts.

Finally his words rewarded my silence. With stoic resolve, he pronounced his interpretation of the scene before him: "All those girls [a meaningful pause] are in their underwear! [Another weighty pause] And that one on the back *is dead!*"

## Left to Die

Sometimes we feel as if we've been stripped of all we hold dear and have been left to die on our life's boat as it struggles to stay afloat on tempestuous seas.

Those must have been the feelings of slave trader John Newton when he was caught in a raging storm on a ship journeying from Africa to England. Sure he would drown in the mountainous waves,

Newton started reading Thomas à Kempis's book *Imitation of Christ*.

The life-threatening experience at sea, coupled with the truths in Kempis's book, eventually led Newton to a point of conversion. He later became a well-known hymn writer. Without that dread storm, Newton might never have turned to the Lord, and we would have been without such inspiring hymns as the much-loved "Amazing Grace."

Jesus wants to rescue us from the dark, angry waters. He wants us to walk the waves with Him to a victorious life. No matter how afraid we are, no matter how strong the wind is blowing, no matter how deep the water, the "I am" of Moses, Peter, and John Newton is still our "I am" today.

## Three Life Rafts

If you're struggling to keep afloat, hold on to these "life rafts" in your heart:

*Life Raft No. 1—Determination*
- Failure is only a temporary setback.
- No one ever achieves a victory without taking a risk.
- Failure is a preparation for success.

*Life Raft No. 2—Examination*
- Ask: Have I fully committed my life to Christ?
- Ask: What actions or attitudes do I have that displease Him?
- Ask: What do I need to release to Him?
- Ask: What has God already told me to do?

*Life Raft No. 3—Mobilization*
- Learn from the storms of life.
- Let the crisis push you up, not pull you down.
- Use your failures as a springboard to victory.

The Christian life that is joyless is a
discredit to God and a disgrace to itself.
—Maltbie D. Babcock

# 6

# ACCEPTING YOUR LOSS AND FOCUSING ON THE ETERNAL

Since we are surrounded by such a great cloud of witnesses, let us throw off everything that hinders and the sin that so easily entangles, and let us run with perseverance the race marked out for us. Let us fix our eyes on Jesus, the author and perfecter of our faith, who for the joy set before him endured the cross, scorning its shame, and sat down at the right hand of the throne of God. Consider him who endured such opposition from sinful men, so that you will not grow weary and lose heart.

—Heb. 12:1-3

Anybody who knew my (Debra's) grandmother Onie White would agree that the woman was nothing short of a *force*. If she was in the room, nay, in the same neighborhood, you knew she was present, and you knew *exactly* what she thought, whether or not you wanted her opinion.

My earliest memories of my grandmother include her coming to visit our home for a week or two. She usually brought her unsalted crackers and other dietary necessities for a person with high cholesterol.

I remember her getting off the Greyhound bus with Zero candy bars for my sister and me. Regardless of her meager income, she always had a big turkey ready for the family at Thanksgiving and Christmas. She loved to cook, and what a cook she was!

After I married Daniel, I knew if Ma White came to spend the night, I would have no ice cream left the next morning. Nobody ever actually saw her devouring the whole container of butter pecan because she got up in the middle of the night, while no one was looking, and finished it off.

Then, of course, there was that moment in church that I described earlier, when I accidentally ripped off her hairnet. She thought I de-netted her on purpose. After the service, when I was collapsing on a nearby pew, howling with laughter, she got irritated at me for laughing so loudly. She always said I laughed too loudly. But everyone says I have *her* laugh.

Life with Ma White was one escapade after another. After receiving a bleak prognosis while lying in the intensive care unit at the hospital, she stated, "Well, looks like I'm a gone goslin'!" And she was.

Early the next morning, she attempted to get out of bed to use the bathroom. The nurses had strictly forbidden her to do so, but since when did that stop Ma White? Her stubborn insistence on moving under her own power led to the collapse of vital arteries around her heart.

My aunt called me early that morning to say that Ma White was dying. I knew I had to be there to bid her farewell. Within an hour I stood with my father and his twin sister beside my grandmother's bed. I held her hand and watched the heart monitor as we exchanged stories of Ma White's exploits. Through tears and laughter, we agreed with the physician that the medication keeping her worn-out heart pumping should be stopped. Soon afterward her heart rate grew slower and slower.

We talked about our good times with her. We laughed. We

cried. And she squeezed my hand a bit. At last the heart monitor showed that Ma White was in her final moments.

My father, my aunt, and I gathered closely around to stroke her forehead and say good-bye. "We love you . . . We'll miss you . . . but we know you're going to be with the Lord."

Even with the heart monitor showing precious few beats and Ma White supposedly "unconscious," she tried to speak to us, but her voice could not form the words. And then she was gone. Her hands grew cold, her face became drawn, but her spirit went to be with God.

I've never experienced the peace in a room that I felt during the moments following her death. I couldn't see angels, but I felt their presence as distinctly as I felt the presence of my father and my aunt. Surely my grandmother was ushered into glory by a host of heavenly beings, singing anthems to the King of Glory.

Days later we looked into her casket to see her as she had been in life—glasses and hairnet ever in place (well, except for that one unforgettable moment!). And again I was overcome by that inexplicable peace that had been my companion at her deathbed.

With my sniffling family surrounding her casket for our moment of private grief, all I could think to say was, "Well, she's a gone goslin'!" We exchanged a last laugh and said good-bye to this woman who had loved the Lord with all her heart.

Every time I pass the frozen turkeys in the grocery store, I think of her. Every time I see a hairnet, I think of her. Every time I drive into her neighborhood, I glimpse her house and think how strange it seems that someone else lives there. Truly, my life was imprinted by the woman everyone called "Ma White."

I would have less wish to go to heaven if I knew that God would not understand a joke.

—Martin Luther

## Exploring Loss

All of us have experienced losses of one kind or another. Many times we think that grieving over loss refers only to dealing with the death of a loved one. But if we think of loss only in terms of death, we've missed some important truths.

Life often presents us with losses that are more devastating than even death. For instance, those who have experienced rejection by a spouse often say that the pain of divorce is worse than if that spouse had died. To see a person as a helpless mental patient, not in his or her right mind, or to watch someone lie in a coma for decades can produce a grief that exceeds death. And there are a host of smaller losses that we may grieve.

When we deny our feelings and don't give ourselves the opportunity to grieve over them, we rob ourselves of the opportunity to build confidence in God's faithfulness.

God wants to meet us in the silence—He wants to whisper to us in those times when no one else knows what to say. He wants to support and comfort us when we're stricken by a catastrophe, whether it's great or small.

## A Variety of Losses

Losses come in a variety of shapes, forms, and sizes, and with differing degrees of intensity. You may be struggling with the loss of your

- Parent
- Spouse
- Child
- Marriage
- Friend
- Childhood
- Fertility
- Job
- Financial security
- Reputation

- Youthful vigor
- Usefulness since retirement
- Childhood innocence

Grief always follows loss. Grief is a universal, complex, and painful process of dealing with and adjusting to loss. Even animals have been known to grieve the loss of a mate or master. This human reaction is a normal and unavoidable part of life; we grieve because we live in a world plagued by sin and death.

Grieving can be a confusing and disorienting process, and one that often takes a great amount of time. After the death of his wife, C. S. Lewis wrote, "In grief, nothing 'stays put.' One keeps on emerging from a phase, but it always recurs. Round and round. Everything repeats."[1]

Grief is not something we get *over*, but rather something we head *through*. And the way we grieve can shape the rest of our lives. If in our grief we cling to God, He will use that journey to deepen and enrich our walk with Him—to give us a new dimension of wisdom and to carve a clearer representation of His image into our heart.

But if we cling to bitterness, unforgiveness, and anger, like some rotting, water-soaked log floating in a river, we will soon become so exhausted—and hardened and helpless—that God will be forever skewed in our mind.

In the comic strip "Shoe," Skyler holds up his report card and says, "I study all night and get a lousy 'C'— and dumb Lenny lucks out with an 'A'!" His father replies, "You may as well get used to it, Skyler . . . life isn't fair. But then, death doesn't have a good track record either."

## Caroline's Song

If you've been around the Church longer than a week, you know that Christians are not exempt from suffering. A tragic example of this is posed in the life of Caroline Sandell-Berg (1832—1903), who penned the well-known hymn "Day by Day."

Caroline was the devoted daughter of a Swedish pastor. When she was 26, she and her father sailed toward Gothenburg. But when the ship lurched, her beloved father fell overboard, and she watched him drown.

Although Caroline had written hymns before this experience, the songs that she wrote with a broken heart seemed to reflect a deeper faith and greater understanding of God's presence in her life.[2]

Her best known song shows that she had learned to depend on God in her grief.

> Day by day, and with each passing moment,
>    Strength I find to meet my trials here.
> Trusting in my Father's wise bestowment,
>    I've no cause for worry or for fear.
> He whose heart is kind beyond all measure
>    Gives unto each day what He deems best,
> Lovingly its part of pain and pleasure,
>    Mingling toil with peace and rest.
>
> Ev'ry day the Lord himself is near me,
>    With a special mercy for each hour.
> All my cares He fain would bear and cheer me,
>    He whose name is Counselor and Pow'r.
> The protection of His child and treasure
>    Is a charge that on himself He laid.
> "As thy days, thy strength shall be in measure,"
>    This the pledge to me He made.
>
> Help me then, in ev'ry tribulation,
>    So to trust Thy promises, O Lord,

> *That I lose not faith's sweet consolation,*
>     *Offered me within Thy holy Word.*
> *Help me, Lord, when toil and trouble meeting,*
>     *E'er to take, as from a Father's hand,*
> *One by one, the days, the moments fleeting,*
>     *Till I reach the promised land.*
>                     —Caroline V. Sandell-Berg

## Acknowledging Grief

Caroline could sing in the storms of her suffering because she knew her Redeemer understood her sorrow. Jesus Christ tasted grief, suffering, and loss when He died on the Cross. The Bible says of Him, "We do not have a high priest who is unable to sympathize with our weaknesses, but we have one who has been tempted in every way, just as we are—yet was without sin" (Heb. 4:15).

Jesus has a firsthand understanding of the things that break our heart. We see how He experienced grief when He mourned the death of His friend Lazarus. The simple verse "Jesus wept" (John 11:35) speaks volumes about the necessity of acknowledging and expressing sorrow.

Weeping has been called the language of the soul. Even the Son of God experienced this language. God is saying to us, "See how my Son, Jesus, responded to loss with tears. Go ahead and weep. Look at my Son. Acknowledge your feelings."

## Waste Management

The acknowledging and releasing of our feelings after a loss is imperative if we're to experience emotional health. Whether the loss involves childhood abuse, our health, relationships, death, or even bankruptcy, we must allow our emotions to flow. Only after the salty waters flow from the soul will God be able to heal us.

Our human tendencies can cause us to bury our emotions and pretend that all is well, when in actuality there's a toxic danger lurking underneath.

Take the following illustration. Fifty years ago we believed that we could bury toxic waste and it would go away. We have since learned better. Buried waste leaks into the water table, contaminating crops, causing death.

Denying a loss and burying grief will do the same thing. Time alone cannot heal the agony of our losses. Therefore, when we hide our torment and wait for time to heal, we are actually intensifying the problem. Buried pain leaks into our emotions, wreaking havoc within our souls. These toxic emotions distort our perceptions of life and taint our relationships. The fascinating thing about emotional contamination is that it can occur without our comprehension. This results in a person whose world seems forever cloudy. A stagnant river of sadness courses through his or her heart and soul.

If we dare to live life to the fullest, we will inevitably experience loss. In a marriage, one spouse will eventually die before the other. If we develop a friendship, there's always the possibility that the relationship will be broken. If we start a new career, there's always a chance that we will fail. But when such losses occur, we have a choice in our reaction.

People who acknowledge their feelings and express their grief begin the journey of hope. Conversely, those who bury their feelings are subject to the effects of "toxic waste."

David writes, "You are my refuge and my shield; I have put my hope in your word. . . . Sustain me according to your promise, and I will live; do not let my hopes be dashed. Uphold me, and I will be delivered; I will always have regard for your decrees" (Ps. 119:114, 116-117). He decided to be open and honest before the Lord. And so must we.

## Grief Traps

Many of the responses to grief that seem the most natural are actually the most harmful. In *The Grief Recovery Book,* James and Frank Clay identify several unhealthful coping strategies people often use when dealing with grief:

**Burying the pain.** As already noted, this only complicates the problem.

**Replacing the loss.** For serious losses, rushing into another venture or relationship, especially remarriage, can be a tragic mistake.

**Grieving alone.** Grieving in community promotes healing. The disciples themselves grieved together after the death of Jesus.

**Giving it time.** Unless time is used to honestly deal with our true feelings, time itself will not cure a gaping wound.

**Living with regret.** A life full of regrets is evidence that we're still focusing on the past. While all of us have times of bemoaning our past choices and actions, we must never become *bound* by regrets. Regrets, like sin and sorrow, can be left at the cross of Jesus Christ.

**Walling up and never trusting again.** This temptation is strongest after betrayal. While betrayal initially leaves us wary, living behind a wall prohibits God from using others to embrace us while we grieve. Cowering behind a wall also prohibits us from ever truly enjoying life again.[3]

He called a little child and had him stand among them. And he said: "I tell you the truth, unless you change and become like little children, you will never enter the kingdom of heaven. Therefore, whoever humbles himself like this child is the greatest in the kingdom of heaven."

—Matt. 18:2-4

We don't have to fall into these six patterns. God wants to strengthen us and help us move from merely existing to living victoriously. He wants us to learn to accept our earthly losses and focus on the eternal.

Children often teach us as much, or more, as we may teach

them. Their simplicity often speaks more wisdom than years of education can provide. At times, a child's pure faith will challenge the most devout adult. And along with their simplicity and faith, they often provide ample moments of humor.

One day my (Debra's) five-year-old son, Brett, said, "I know what Jesus' last name is. It's 'Amen,' because we say, 'In Jesus' name —Amen.'"

Then there was the time the preacher spoke about the fact that "many are called, but few are chosen" (Matt. 22:14, KJV). Another mother asked her son about the sermon topic, he answered, "Many are cold, and a few are frozen."

When asked to write letters to God, some witty and wonderful children provided the following nuggets of theological humor:

Dear God,

Instead of letting people die and having to make new ones, why don't You just keep the ones You have?

Amy

Dear God,

Maybe Cain and Abel would not kill each other so much if they had their own rooms. It works with my brother.

Larry

Dear God,

I bet it is very hard for You to love all of everybody in the whole world. There are only 4 people in our family, and I can never do it.

Nan

Dear God,

I would like to live 900 years like the guy in the Bible.

Love,
Chris

Dear God,

Did you really mean "Do unto others as they do unto you"?

Because if you did, then I'm going to fix my brother.

Darla

Dear God,

What is it like when you die? Nobody will tell me. I just want to know.

I don't want to do it.

Your friend,<br>Mike

When we take a deeper look at those cute letters, we'll discover they actually speak to the child in us. For example, if we're honest, we'll all admit that deep inside, we don't *want* to die . . . don't *want* to experience losses . . . we *desperately wish* our world were free of disease, death, divorce, depression, and despair.

But that's not the world in which we live. And when losses come, we will deal with them much more wisely if we're equipped with sound, biblical steps to direct us through the grieving process. Instead of falling into those traps that result in walling up and never trusting again, we can place our childlike faith in God and His healing power to help us accept the loss and focus on what cannot be lost.

If you or someone you know has endured a loss, the following suggestions will assist you.

**1. You will accept the loss and focus on the eternal if you believe that God will bring good from your loss.**

> We know that in all things God works for the good of those who love him *(Rom. 8:28).*

The motion picture *A River Runs Through It* tells the story of a family named Maclean who lived in Montana early in the 20th century. In the movie, the father, a Presbyterian minister, is stern but loving. His wife is supportive and nurturing. They have two sons, Norman and Paul.

We meet the Maclean family when the boys are young, squirming in the front row while their father preaches in church. We watch them grow up through childhood, stormy adolescence, and cross the threshold into adulthood. Norman is cautious and studious. Eventually he goes to college and then becomes a writer and professor. Paul is the daredevil, a man with quick wit and a winning smile.

However, the real protagonist of the story is the river that runs through their part of Montana. That river becomes the focal point of their family life and the catalyst for everything significant that takes place in their individual lives. Walking along the river's banks on Sunday afternoons, the father forges a relationship with his young boys—turning over rocks, teaching them about the world, about life, and about the God who created it all. After studies, the boys run to the river, where sibling rivalry and brotherly affection flourish as they fish for trout in that gurgling water.

When adolescence arrives and the boys must prove their manhood, they take a death-defying ride down the rapids in a stolen boat. A little later on the river, young Paul makes a name for himself as the finest fly fisherman in the territory. When Norman comes back from college, searching for himself and his roots, he goes to the river to fish alongside his brother.

The Maclean family knows failure and success, laughter and fighting, change and disappointment, but the river is always there. That river is a major defining force and a spiritual center of the family. If not for the river, Montana would have been a wilderness, their home simply four walls and a roof, their lives just sound and fury.

A different river runs through the lives of Christians: *the will of God.* Even though life's clouds and storms sometimes block our view of that will, it is there, nonetheless, weaving amid our lives. And we have a choice, whether to allow God's will to flow freely —including over the territories of our losses—or to build dams of doubt.

**2. You will accept the loss and focus on the eternal if you get on with life!**

Do you not know that in a race all the runners run, but only one gets the prize? Run in such a way as to get the prize. Everyone who competes in the games goes into strict training. They do it to get a crown that will not last; but we do it to get a crown that will last forever *(1 Cor. 9:24-25)*.

Since we are surrounded by such a great cloud of witnesses, let us throw off everything that hinders and the sin that so easily entangles, and let us run with perseverance the race marked out for us. Let us fix our eyes on Jesus, the author and perfecter of our faith, who for the joy set before him endured the cross, scorning its shame, and sat down at the right hand of the throne of God. Consider him who endured such opposition from sinful men, so that you will not grow weary and lose heart *(Heb. 12:1-3)*.

Jim Ryun, now a member of the United States Congress, was an Olympic athlete in the 1960s. His goal—what he wanted more than anything in all the world—was a gold medal at the Olympics. He trained four years to reach that goal.

In 1968 he went to the Olympics in Mexico City, whose altitude is 8,000 feet. Since he had not trained in that high of an altitude, his breathing was affected, and he came in second. "But I won't quit," he insisted.

For four more years he trained to go to the 1972 Olympics in Munich, Germany. Everyone thought he would win the mile run. As he was competing in the preliminary run, every eye was on Jim. As usual, he lagged behind, waiting to use his "great finishing kick," where he would pass everyone in the last lap, or half-lap, and win the race.

Jim was running gracefully with a good stride and good wind—when suddenly he and a fellow runner tripped over each other. Stunned, both fell to the cinder. They lay there on the track, trying to figure out exactly what happened. The other runners were now about 200 yards ahead. Catching up with even the last man was impossible.

Eight years of training had come to naught, eight years of rising before dawn and running miles a day. All the labor. All those dreams of the gold medal. And there Jim lay on the cinder. The other runner got up, dusted himself off, and walked to the infield to sit down and watch the race. But Jim got up and kept running. He did not catch up. He finished a distant last. But he *did* finish.

Like Jim Ryun, we must keep running. When we experience loss, we must be willing to stay in the race, to get on with our lives—even if we're aching from our injuries. Notice Jim's last name is actually Run, with a *y* added. That *y* represents "you." You're a runner—whether you finish last or first. Whether or not you receive applause, you must keep running. With Jesus at your side, the Holy Spirit empowering your feet, and God the Father urging you toward the finish line, *you* are a winner!

> *Dare to run with our eyes fixed on Jesus,*
> *Following the footsteps of the One who's gone before us.*
> *Dare to run in the power of His Spirit,*
> *Called to be victors in a race already won; dare to run.* *
> —Harlan Moore and Joel W. Smith

**3. You will accept the loss and focus on the eternal if you do not withdraw.**

A new command I give you: Love one another. As I have loved you, so you must love one another *(John 13:34).*

Norman Vincent Peale and his brother, Bob, were very close. When Bob died, Dr. Peal was inconsolable. However, despite his grief, he chose not to withdraw from his life or his acquaintances. Instead, he continued in his speaking for the Foundation for Christian Living.

---

*© 1989 Lillenas Publishing Company (administered by the Copyright Company, Nashville, TN). All rights reserved. International copyright secured. Used by permission.

In the midst of his reaching out and loving others, Dr. Peale had an unusual experience. He writes, "One day I was speaking to a meeting of employees of the Foundation when suddenly I 'saw' him, clearly and distinctly, striding across a plaza between our building and his house. It was all perfectly real. He looked to be about 40 years of age, in the prime of life, healthy and energetic. He waved with the old-time gesture and the same smile that I knew so well and seemed to say, 'It's all right, Deacon. It's all right.'"[4]

Withdrawing from loved ones and life often cuts us off from the very source of healing that God wants to use on our behalf.

**4. You will accept the loss and focus on the eternal if you ask the Holy Spirit to heal your hurts.**

> Be merciful to me, LORD, for I am faint; O LORD, heal me, for my bones are in agony. My soul is in anguish. How long, O LORD, how long? Turn, O LORD, and deliver me; save me because of your unfailing love *(Ps. 6:2-4)*.

Healing is a process. Healing doesn't mean that you will never carry scars; but with the help of the Holy Spirit, those scars can be the beauty marks of a miracle rather than memories of agony.

This is not a simple one- or two-step quick fix. Healing can be a complex process. After a tragic loss, life is never the same. But with the help of the Holy Spirit, we can move forward, admitting and overcoming pain, not burying it.

Healing is both spiritual and physical. Our spirit starts the journey that will never be complete until we surrender the throne of our lives to the Holy Spirit. If we struggle with God over His control, we will only rob ourselves of the complete healing He has to offer.

### Ode to Devastation

*Hello, my friend.*
*Don't be surprised*
*That I call you friend.*

*Because of you, God has taught me . . .*
*Oh, how He has taught me . . .*

*To cling to Him,*
*To taste true forgiveness,*
*To understand.*
*Being put back together piece by piece*
*By the Holy Creator.*

*Because of you, God has taught me . . .*
*To trust Him despite the circumstances,*
*To trust Him when His answer is no,*
*To trust Him simply because He is God . . .*
*He is wise . . . He is love . . . He is sovereign.*

*Because of you, God has taught me . . .*
*To unconditionally love*
*Those who almost destroyed me . . .*
*To accept His best for me,*
*Even if that means my own pain . . .*
*To comfort the devastated*
*Because I have been intimate with you.*

*So thank you, Devastation.*
*Thanks for your scarring footprints*
*Upon my life,*
*The footprints in which Jesus Christ*
*Tread after you,*
*Transforming each scar*
*To joy and beauty.*

—Debra White Smith

5. **You will accept the loss and focus on the eternal if you stand on the promises of Scripture.**

Here are 12 scriptural promises you can claim:

- **God is always with you:** "Never will I leave you" (Heb. 13:5).
- **God is your shield:** "I am your shield" (Gen. 15:1).
- **God is all-powerful:** "I will strengthen you" (Isa. 41:10).

- **God will meet your needs:** "The LORD is my shepherd, I shall not be in want" (Ps. 23:1).
- **God's guidance is reliable:** "When he has brought out all his own, he goes ahead of them" (John 10:4).
- **God has a plan for your life:** "'I know the plans I have for you,' declares the LORD, 'plans to prosper you and not to harm you, plans to give you hope and a future'" (Jer. 29:11). *(Note: This famous scripture came to Israel during a time of exile.)*
- **God's peace is restful:** "Come to me, all you who are weary and burdened, and I will give you rest" (Matt. 11:28).
- **God cleanses you from *all* sin:** "If we confess our sins, he is faithful and just and will forgive us our sins and purify us from all unrighteousness" (1 John 1:9).
- **God gives good gifts:** "No good thing does he withhold from those whose walk is blameless" (Ps. 84:11).
- **God is merciful:** "For the sake of his great name the LORD will not reject his people" (1 Sam. 12:22).
- **God's guidance is perfect:** "He guides the humble in what is right and teaches them his way" (Ps. 25:9).
- **God's calling is clear:** "We know that in all things God works for the good of those who love him, who have been called according to his purpose" (Rom. 8:28).

> *Standing on the promises of Christ, my King!*
> *Thro' eternal ages let His praises ring.*
> *"Glory in the highest!" I will shout and sing,*
> *Standing on the promises of God.*
>
> *Standing on the promises that cannot fail!*
> *When the howling storms of doubt and fear assail,*
> *By the living Word of God I shall prevail,*
> *Standing on the promises of God.*

*Standing on the promises of Christ, the Lord,*
*Bound to Him eternally by love's strong cord,*
*Overcoming daily with the Spirit's Sword,*
*Standing on the promises of God.*

—R. Kelso Carter

**6. You will accept the loss and focus on the eternal if you invest your life in bringing hope to others.**

Praise be to the God and Father of our Lord Jesus Christ, the Father of compassion and the God of all comfort, who comforts us in all our troubles, so that we can comfort those in any trouble with the comfort we ourselves have received from God. For just as the sufferings of Christ flow over into our lives, so also through Christ our comfort overflows *(2 Cor. 1:3-5).*

This very book is an example of that principle. Both of us have known grief up close and personally. Between the two of us, we have experienced a wide range of losses. And we can write with the confidence of having lived what we are writing—not only exploring the awful devastation of loss but also proclaiming the victorious deliverance found through Jesus Christ our Lord.

Without Him, life is a journey through a long, dark tunnel with no light at the end. But as fellow strugglers, we boldly proclaim to you that focusing on Him is focusing on the light—a light that brings healing and hope.

Here are some practical ways you can help others discover that kind of hope:

- **Be a volunteer.** Give some of your time and energy to a hospital, school, boys' home, girls' home, nursing home, crisis pregnancy center, any kind of shelter (for the homeless, battered and abused women, or even the animal shelter).
- **Appoint yourself as the official card-sender at your church.** Send cards to everyone who is sick or has experienced a loss.
- **Adopt a friend.** Take a needy kid golfing, fishing, swimming, or shopping. "Adopt" a single mom and/or father, and help with the kids. If possible, you could actually legally adopt a

child. Thousands of children need homes. Now, both couples and singles can adopt, and the age range for adoptive parents is from the 20s to the mid-50s.

- **Laugh a little.** When Dan Jansen brought home a gold medal from the Winter Olympics in 1994, he did so with the help of a sports psychologist named James Loehr. In addition to the routine regimen of proper training, healthful eating, and adequate rest, Jansen was also instructed to lighten up and laugh more. Dr. Loehr noted studies that prove humor relaxes the body and relieves stress. He said a lot can be learned from children in that research shows children laugh an unbelievable 400 times a day on average. This is compared to adults, who average only 15 laughs a day. The writer of Prov. 15:15 was right—"The cheerful heart has a continual feast."

- **Call or E-mail someone.** Get in the habit of contacting people who need encouragement, at least one per day. Laugh with them. Cry with them. Just *be* there for them.

- **Make a prayer list.** List by name those you know who are grieving, and pray for them daily. Notify those on your list of your prayers, and be sure to put yourself on the list as well.

- **Prepare a meal.** Identify someone, perhaps in your church, who has experienced a loss, and prepare a home-cooked meal for him or her. If you don't have any culinary skills, you may want to take the person out for a meal or for dessert and coffee.

- **Start a Sunday School class or Bible study.** Invite some friends or loved ones who have recently experienced a loss to a Bible study that focuses on recovery.

- **Visit your local hospital maternity ward.** Leave an anonymous note for each set of new parents, explaining that you have placed their child's name on your prayer list. Or donate inexpensive Bibles for all the babies born on the birthday of that special someone you lost.

- **Visit a local jail or prison.** Get the name of an inmate from a friend or associate, and request permission to visit him or her. Then visit the families of the inmate if possible.

- **Appoint yourself as the official anonymous encourager at work.** Leave anonymous notes of encouragement to fellow employees.
- **Write encouraging poetry, songs, articles, or books.** Your church bulletin editor would probably be delighted to print a few poems.

Choosing one or two ways to focus on comforting and encouraging others will open new doors of blessing for you. You may say, "But I just don't *feel* like encouraging others right now." Do it anyway!

Often our good feelings follow our good actions. If we wait for our feelings to dictate what we do, we'll wait around our whole lives.

When we make Christ our reason for living,
no matter what or who we lose,
our reason for living still lives!

—Debra White Smith

# 7
# OVERCOMING LONELINESS

A father to the fatherless, a defender of widows,
is God in his holy dwelling. God sets the lonely in
families, he leads forth the prisoners with singing.
—Ps. 68:5-6

One night I (Stan) was called to visit the home of a man who said he wanted to get right with God. I was only 25 years old at the time and was pastoring in southern Ohio. In my youthful vigor for the Lord, I never imagined the dangerous situation into which I was about to step.

When I arrived at the man's apartment, the dingy room smelled of alcohol, and I noticed a bottle of Thunderbird wine clutched in his hand. He was dressed in well-worn army fatigues, and his body odor mingled with the odor of the wine. Hesitantly, I took a seat in a dilapidated chair as he recalled his experiences as a Vietnam War soldier.

A nervous feeling began crawling up my spine as he alternately wept, got angry, pounded the coffee table, laughed, and told stories about his war days. While he was talking, I noticed a lot of things about him—his unshaven face, his scraggly hair, and his wary eyes. I also noticed a Bible on the couch—with a handgun under it. My palms moistened, and I began planning a swift exit.

The man continued his tirade, telling agonizing stories of having to kill people in the war. I tried to share my faith with him, but that only irritated him. He began to rail at me, and then he railed at God. Although my stomach was churning, I offered to pray with him. He stubbornly refused.

With all the courage I could muster, I stood to leave. But he picked up the handgun, pointed it at me, and ordered me back to my chair. I may have been young, but I certainly wasn't foolish—I did what the man said!

By now, not only was he voicing his rage, loneliness, and disappointment with God and our government, but he was also carelessly waving that handgun around as if it were a toy. Through broken sobs, he explained that the alcohol was his way to overcome his problems. He continued to take swigs from the Thunderbird wine bottle until he ultimately fell asleep.

I slowly began my exit. Walking to the door, I turned around and took one last look at that tormented soul, gripping the wine bottle in one hand and the handgun in the other. Though I had felt like a hostage, one look at him evidenced who the real hostage was. I silently prayed that he would find release from his demons of hostility, depression, and loneliness.

> The saving grace of America lies in the fact that the overwhelming majority of Americans are possessed of two great qualities—
> a sense of humor and a sense of proportion.
> —Franklin D. Roosevelt

## Hostages of Loneliness

The late Mother Teresa said, "The most terrible poverty is loneliness and the feeling of being unwanted." Millions of people are hostages to loneliness, just like that war veteran was a prisoner of his anger and hostility. An estimated one-fourth of our nation experiences regular levels of isolation and loneliness. Joan Nielsen, a social worker in Tucson, Arizona, said loneliness is the biggest problem of most retirees she sees:

> They leave their children and social contacts up North and come here not knowing a soul. I see people who never leave their home except to go to the grocery and the doctor. They just let things happen. Some start drinking heavily. One day they run out of money and have no place to live. An upper-class housing development here brags about "the grin of satisfaction" among their elderly residents. We social workers say, "The grin comes from drinking too much gin." A study among the occupants showed the average household there consuming five quarts of liquor per week.[1]

Loneliness, with its accompanying feeling of emptiness, is a common condition—from the famous to the infamous, from the richest to the poorest, from the elderly to the youthful. But loneliness is largely unseen. Lee Strobel says, "There's one admission that people are loath to make, whether they're a star on television or someone who fixes televisions in a repair shop. Most of us are just too embarrassed to say those two little words: *I'm lonely.*"[2]

## A Hole in the Heart

A one-time leading Hollywood actress told *USA Today*, "It sounds so trendy . . . but I believe a lot of us feel a kind of hole in our heart—an unfocused ache that's fixed by some people eating too much, for others with free base. In my case, I'm a romantic junkie."

According to United States Senate Chaplain Lloyd Ogilvie, "Loneliness is not isolation: it's insulation. It's the fear of knowing and being known."[3] Actor Eddie Murphy told *People* magazine, "I feel something's missing. I don't think there's anyone who feels like there isn't something missing in their life. No matter how much money you make, or how many cars or houses you have, or how many people you make happy, life isn't perfect for anybody."[4]

Late rock star Jerry Garcia was one in a long line of 1960s celebrities who felt there was something missing. Such feelings led many of those lonely multimillionaires into a tragic ending to their tormented lives.

## Created for Intimacy with God

Though loneliness can be a tragic trap into which people of all social strata can fall, God did not create us to be held its hostage. He created us to become intimate with Him in a loving and accepting relationship. And He intends for us to share that intimacy with others. Until we learn intimacy with Him, we will find that loneliness does indeed forever hold us hostage.

As Eddie Murphy stated so accurately, "something's missing."

Each of us was created with a piece missing from the center of our hearts—a piece in the shape of a cross. Only through the provisions of Calvary's cross will we find true release from feelings of loneliness and emptiness.

While even the most devout among us might experience *seasons* of loneliness, God never intended for us to live a *lifestyle* of loneliness.

It has been said that when they thrust the spear into Christ's side, causing blood and water to come out, it was an indication that Jesus literally died of a broken heart.[5]

Jesus Christ died brokenhearted so we don't have to. He not only bore our sin on that terrible cross but also bore our sorrow and our loneliness.

## Finding Solace in the Savior

With Christ as our Savior, we have the amazing privilege of sensing His presence with us every single moment of every single day, regardless of what life might bring. Even when we're saying, "The harder I laugh, the deeper I hurt," our souls can find solace in Him. We can gain comfort in knowing that He experienced loneliness and desolation in a far greater sense than we ever will. We also gain comfort in realizing that He is forever willing to help us carry the burden of our pain and loneliness.

Author and musician Jerry Brecheisen speaks of sitting beside his aged mother, who had given nearly 50 years of her life in music ministries throughout North America. Her partner in that ministry, her beloved husband, had recently passed away, and she was left in ill health. As he sat with her, Jerry reminisced about his days of traveling on the road with his parents in their ministry. He put in the compact disc player some piano music he had recently recorded and then sat quietly so she could listen.

Suddenly the lyrics sung by the backup singers filled the room—and filled his heart until tears raced down his cheeks. They were these words from Frank Graeff's great gospel song:

> *Does Jesus care when my heart is pained*
> *Too deeply for mirth and song,*
> *As the burdens press, and the cares distress,*
> *And the way grows weary and long?*
>
> *Does Jesus care when my way is dark*
> *With a nameless dread and fear?*
> *As the daylight fades into deep night shades,*
> *Does he care enough to be near?*
>
> *Does Jesus care when I've said good-bye*
> *To the dearest on earth to me,*
> *And my sad heart aches till it nearly breaks?*
> *Is it aught to Him? Does He see?*
>
> *O yes, He cares;*
> *I know He cares!*
> *His heart is touched with my grief.*
> *When the days are weary,*
> *The long nights dreary,*
> *I know my Savior cares.*

—Frank E. Graeff

Jerry says a heavenly thought gripped his heart like a vise: "God has not forgotten my mother. And He knows how much I miss my father. He cares enough to come and sit with us on a couch in a tiny den and sing a song of hope to our hearts."[6]

You, too, may be lonely. But you're not alone. The ever-living Christ is in the room. Hopefully He is there as your Savior, one to whom you have dedicated your life. But most assuredly, He is there as the dearest friend you will ever know.

## Exploring Loneliness

Recently Stan received an E-mail listing the top 10 reasons God created Eve. Here they are:

10. God worried that Adam would always be lost in the Garden, because men hate to ask for directions.

9. God knew that Adam would one day need someone to hand him the television remote control. (Men don't want to see what's on television—they want to see *what else* is on!)

8. God knew that Adam would never buy a new fig leaf when his wore out, and Eve would have to get one for him.

7. God knew that Adam would never make a doctor's appointment for himself.

6. God knew that Adam would never remember which night was garbage night.

5. God knew that if the world was to be populated, men would never be able to handle childbearing.

4. As "keeper of the Garden," Adam would never remember where he put his tools.

3. The Scripture account of Creation indicates Adam needed someone to blame his troubles on when God caught him hiding in the Garden.

2. As the Bible says, "It is not good for the man to be alone."

1. When God finished the creation of Adam, He stepped back, scratched His head, and said, "I can do better than that!"

And in all fairness to Adam, here are Debra's top 10 reasons *Eve* needed *Adam:*

10. God knew Eve would have trouble changing her own flat tires.

9. God knew Eve would need someone to ask about her hairstyle, only to do exactly the opposite of what Adam suggested.

8. God knew Eve would need someone to witness her changing her mind over and over and over again.

7. God knew Eve would never be on time without Adam to stand nearby and tap his watch.

6. God knew Eve would need someone from whom to hide all those bargain clothes she put on the credit card.

5. God knew when the toilet stopped up, Eve would need someone to whom she could hand the plunger.

4. God figured Eve needed someone to drive the car, because there isn't a vanity mirror on the driver's side.

3. God wasn't about to place Eve in that garden alone. Who would kill the snakes?

2. Since women say about 25,000 words a day, God wanted Eve to have someone to whom she could talk at least half of her daily word count before starting on Him.

1. God knew Eve needed someone to throw things at during labor.

In fact, God did create human beings for each other. We are lonely without a significant other in our life. But loneliness is more than just being alone. Loneliness is a feeling of being separated from others and isolated even in a crowd, a sense of restlessness, an intense desire to be needed and to be wanted by someone—*anyone.*

## Types of Loneliness

There are four types of loneliness: emotional, social, spiritual, and situational.

*Emotional loneliness* often surfaces due to a deep injury that destroyed self-esteem and caused the person to block himself or herself off from others. Such a person is often distant in relationships. When talking with an emotionally lonely person, he or she may seem to be mentally and physically present but far away in his or her heart. The only answer for emotional loneliness is emotional healing from God Almighty.

*Social loneliness* occurs when the only dates on our calendar are the preprinted days of the month. In a cartoon, Ziggy finds himself in such a dilemma. He opens his mailbox to see only cobwebs. He turns on the television set to hear the announcer say, "Welcome to Lonely Hearts Theater." Ziggy sneezes and hears an echoing "Achoo." He gets a puzzled look on his face and says, "You never realize how empty and hollow your life is until one day you sneeze and it echoes!"

Social loneliness often occurs when we've chosen not to interact with others. People who are socially lonely often wonder why they're not invited out more or why they're not included in "the group." In reality, social loneliness can be alleviated by letting down social barriers. One way is to get involved with a church fellowship or some other special-interest group. An individual who reaches out to others in genuine love will find his or her social calendar slowly filling up.

*Spiritual loneliness* is the separation from God, which Adam and Eve experienced when they hid from the Lord in the Garden of Eden. Any individual participating in a lifestyle of disobedience to God will be plagued by this loneliness.

Only through a personal relationship with Jesus Christ can spiritual loneliness be eliminated. However, this spiritual friendship involves more than a token admission of Christ as Savior and transcends a habitual Sunday morning church trip followed by a cafeteria "house special."

Forming a spiritual friendship with the Lord includes long and significant talks (prayer), reading correspondence (Bible study), mutual helping (service), and an active respect for Christ's opinion (obedience).

Spiritual loneliness exists in direct proportion to the level of our consecration to God. Only a heart fully abandoned to God experiences the spiritual passion of a love affair with the Lord. Once this happens, our token admission of salvation turns into a glorious testimony of divine grace. Our "habitual trip to church" becomes "I can't wait until the next service!" And our "head knowledge" of Scripture turns to "I can't get enough of God's Word!"

Until the problem of spiritual loneliness is addressed, social loneliness and emotional loneliness cannot be completely overcome.

*Situational loneliness* stems from a combination of the other three—emotional, social, and spiritual. We may do everything within our power to live close to the Heavenly Father, to reach out to others socially, and to pursue emotional healing and intimacy but still find ourselves in a situation that produces loneliness. The following situations depict common causes and cures for loneliness:

- **The loneliness of sin.** In our desires to follow the Lord, we're sometimes caught in an instance of human failing. The prescription for this situation is *immediate* confession and repentance. Allowing sin to creep into our lives—and stay there—ultimately will result in chronic spiritual loneliness.

- **The loneliness of leadership.** Stepping forward as a leader often alienates us from those we're actually leading. They often look up to the leader for guidance and support and consequently distance themselves from him or her. That leaves the leader looking for someone with whom he or she can relate on a personal level. The cure for leadership loneliness is to find fellow leaders with whom intimacy can be shared.

- **The loneliness of success.** Often when an individual achieves success in any measure, his or her peers may become envious. While this should not happen among Christians, it nonetheless does happen. The secret to overcoming the loneliness of success lies in staying humble before the Lord and being down-to-earth with peers. Individuals are less likely to remain envious of someone who is untainted by success and treats everyone as an equal.

- **The loneliness of separation.** If we are away from a spouse or loved one, this type of loneliness is inevitable. However, some steps can be taken to alleviate that loneliness, such as frequent contact through phone, faxes, or E-mail.

  But sometimes that distance is made permanent by death. When a loved one passes, only God in His time can truly fill that vacancy. After my (Debra's) friend Frances Shaw lost her husband, she eventually could say to me, "I'm alone, but not lonely."

- **The loneliness of uncertainty.** Admitting uncertainty often leaves us emotionally vulnerable. Pretending we have no insecurities or uncertainties is an easy trap to fall into. This pretending not only distances us from others but also intensifies our feelings of loneliness. The remedy for the loneliness of uncertainty is to find a friend in whom we can confide without feeling as if we will be scorned. Often a nonjudgmental, listening ear helps relieve uncertainties and loneliness.

The irony of the human condition is that too often we pretend to have it all together. Human beings actually spend a lot of time covering the emotions and concerns that everyone around them is experiencing. We're often afraid that we're the only ones with such feelings. But the truth is that most of our emotions are common.

## The Lonely Hearts Club

A young man sent his picture to a lonely hearts club. A week later he received a reply. Opening the letter, he read these words, "Dear Sir, We're not *that* lonely!"

Consider the many Bible characters who *were* that lonely. They knew loneliness personally:

- **Job:** "My kinsmen have gone away; my friends have forgotten me" (Job 19:14).

- **David:** "How long, O LORD? Will you forget me forever? How long will you hide your face from me?" (Ps. 13:1).
- **Jeremiah:** "I never sat in the company of revelers, never made merry with them; I sat alone because your hand was on me and you had filled me with indignation" (Jer. 15:17).
- **Solomon:** "If one falls down, his friend can help him up. But pity the man who falls and has no one to help him up!" (Eccles. 4:10).
- **Jesus:** "About the ninth hour Jesus cried out in a loud voice, *'Eloi, Eloi, lama sabachthani?'*—which means, 'My God, my God, why have you forsaken me?'" (Matt. 27:46).

These Bible greats also provide us with a clear picture of restoration. Through God's grace, Job overcame his loneliness and desolation. David understood the completeness of God's forgiveness and the comfort of His presence. And Jesus Christ, who tasted death and loneliness for us all, rose the victor over the grave. He walked the darkest side of loneliness. And we can be assured that no matter how dry and lifeless our souls may seem, Jesus is ready and able to breathe His presence upon us anew and teach us how to be overcomers. "Be strong and courageous. Do not be terrified; do not be discouraged, for the LORD your God will be with you wherever you go" (Josh. 1:9).

Don't let [loneliness] kill you—let the church help!

—Church bulletin

## Overcoming Loneliness

Several years ago I (Stan) experienced a time of great loneliness. I was in a large denominational board meeting as a pastor representative and a vital issue was being hotly debated. Finally a roll call vote was required. The chairperson called each member by name and asked him or her to respond with a yes or no. The pressure was high to vote yes, but I felt strongly that I should vote no.

Praying that I wouldn't be alone, I waited while 27 other board members voted in the affirmative. When my turn came to vote, I gritted my teeth and voted a firm no.

My palms were sweating like a junior high school student on a first date (with his mother driving the car).

I shook all over like a 90-year-old rock-and-roll singer.

Perspiration beaded my upper lip like a last-question contestant on *Who Wants to Be a Millionaire?*

As an adult, I've never felt so alone in all my life. In the years following that meeting, many have affirmed me, including the general superintendent who served as the board chairperson. Many of the members said they wished they had voted the way they felt the Lord was leading, not just out of loyalty or being pressured. Yet at the time, I was completely alone.

Enduring the loneliness that may come in defending a principle is difficult. We live in a society in which many are forced to defend principles—and they suffer lonely alienation as a result.

Here are 10 ways to cope when you feel alone in the world.

**1. Be honest with yourself; admit that loneliness may be a result of your actions.** "Act with courage, and may the LORD be with those who do well" (2 Chron. 19:11). To people with no moral compass, doing right often looks like the wrong thing to do. Our "character by convenience" age has a hard time processing "character by choice."

The Bible says, "The man without the Spirit does not accept the things that come from the Spirit of God, for they are foolishness to him, and he cannot understand them, because they are spiritually discerned" (1 Cor. 2:14).

If you're going to live for God and do what's right, there will be times when you'll be the lone ranger. If you can admit that to yourself in advance of your actions, then the loneliness of being separated from the crowd won't come as such a shock.

**2. Be strengthened in your relationship with Christ.** The apostle Paul wrote, "I can do everything through him who gives me strength"

(Phil. 4:13). The one who asked you to be separated from the attitudes and actions of the world also promised to be with you always. The Lord Jesus Christ will never ask you to be something that His grace will not equip you to be. He will never ask you to go somewhere without accompanying you on the journey.

**3. Accept the things that cannot be changed.** Again, Paul said, "I have learned to be content whatever the circumstances" (Phil. 4:11). Life is filled with inevitable things. For instance, a lonely widower will never be able to bring back his deceased wife. A woman whose husband has divorced her and married another woman will not be able to reverse her husband's choices. However, the Lord is able to provide a deep peace and an acceptance of the situation as it stands. Only when we stop looking at the past will we be able to embrace the future.

**4. Be alert to the things that *can* be changed.** "Wait for the LORD; be strong and take heart and wait for the LORD" (Ps. 27:14). Take the time to ask the Lord to show you what He wants you to change, and await His answers. He might surprise you! The very boldness of your actions may bring appreciative admirers into your life. Pray for the courage to do what God says. Do something—make a difference in someone's life. Contribute boldly to the needs of your community.

**5. Be positive.** The Bible says, "Whatever is noble, whatever is right, whatever is pure, whatever is lovely, whatever is admirable—if anything is excellent or praiseworthy—think about such things" (Phil. 4:8). People usually gravitate to individuals who are positive. Look for the good in every situation.

Join organizations that have a positive cause: a small church group, civic organization, or some other organization that aids the needy. Develop a sense of humor. Even in dire circumstances, there's usually something that will cause a laugh or two.

**6. Be aware of God's help.** "God has said, 'Never will I leave you; never will I forsake you.' So we say with confidence, 'The Lord is my helper; I will not be afraid. What can man do to me?'" (Heb.

13:5-6). According to Lloyd Ogilvie, "Our loneliness is a 'homing instinct.' Intimate communion with Him is our home."[7] We will never know an end to loneliness without first relying upon our Creator.

7. **Be on the move.** "Trust in the LORD and do good; dwell in the land and enjoy safe pasture" (Ps. 37:3). A soft drink company many years ago advertised its product as one that produces "the pause that refreshes." But in actuality, the pause doesn't always refresh! Someone without a worthy goal, a purpose, and a plan is often most vulnerable to times of depressing loneliness.

8. **Be joyful.** "Delight yourself in the LORD and he will give you the desires of your heart" (Ps. 37:4). Make a decision to enjoy the journey. As a young father traveling with my family, I (Stan) noticed that my children's attitude changed for the better when they spent more time looking out the window than focusing on reasons to fuss inside the car!

Spend more time looking out the window. Joy is a matter of choice. Have you noticed that lonely people are most often joyless people? They've made a "surrender" in their spirit. They've decided to "fuss" rather than "focus."

9. **Be fully committed to God's agenda.** "Commit your way to the LORD; trust in him and he will do this" (Ps. 37:5). As we've noticed, rebellion against the will of God results in loneliness. We live in a world that for the most part cares little about the agenda that God has outlined in His Word. The world likes to call attention to God's "don'ts." But, in fact, there are as many "dos" as there are "don'ts." If you'll commit yourself to "doing the dos," you'll have little time left to dwell on the "don'ts." His "dos" include sharing the gospel, feeding the hungry, meeting the needs of the poor, and so forth.

10. **Be still.** "Be still before the LORD and wait patiently for him; do not fret when men succeed in their ways, when they carry out their wicked schemes" (Ps. 37:7). My friend Talmadge Johnson told of a man who stopped to watch a Little League baseball game. He asked one of the players what the score was.

"We're losing 18-0" was the youngster's answer.

"Well, I must say, you don't look discouraged," the man responded.

"Discouraged?" the boy said with a puzzled look. "Why should we be? We haven't been to bat yet!"[8]

When the loneliness of living for God and for good in this kind of world settles over your soul, remember: God's people have last bat. "Be still." Listen for the powerful words of affirmation that the Holy Spirit will bring to your heart if you simply listen.

## Too Alive to Be Lonely!

I (Debra) have a wonderful friend, Rob Hubbard, who is an amazing example of someone who could easily allow life's circumstances to drown him in loneliness. Rob was permanently blinded as an infant. Despite his blindness, he lives alone with the help of an elaborate computer system that talks to him.

All of his friends know him as "the computer whiz." Even sighted people often call Rob and ask his input when their computers are giving them problems. If I call with a computer problem, he usually insists something preposterous like, "Debra, you've *got* to read your instructions!" Once Rob had to manually fix the computer for a friend *who could see!* Before he left, Rob said, "You sighted infidel! You don't need those eyes as much as you think you do!"

One day I asked Rob why he didn't get a Seeing Eye dog, and he told me he didn't want one. "A dog would be too much trouble." He walks anywhere he wants to without one. Presently, Rob flies all over the United States *alone* to assist sight-impaired individuals in setting up and running their own computer systems. I recently received an E-mail from him. He was in Michigan, and he said he was wandering around a luxury hotel getting lost. "But you've got to get lost before you can get found!" he wrote.

Although Rob has never been married, the idea of sitting at home and feeling sorry for himself leaves him irate. He has no plans to marry until he finds the woman God intends for him. "I don't want a woman who will feel sorry for me or act like my mother," he insists. And heaven help the woman who does!

Lonely? The word doesn't enter Rob Hubbard's vocabulary. This man has an intimate relationship with Jesus Christ. He's too alive to be lonely. He has places to go, people to "see," planes to catch, and things to do! That also includes being a counselor at a camp for visually impaired children. "Too many times blind people feel sorry for themselves," Rob says. In short, he doesn't have time for that. "Loneliness is a choice," he claims. "I choose *not* to be lonely."

## Reach Out!

Poet Henry Wadsworth Longfellow pictured what we often experience in daily life when he compared life to two ships at sea passing each other during the night. There is a brief light or sound to acknowledge each other's presence, and then quickly the darkness returns. That brief passing may describe our human experience if we don't take specific steps to avoid such a dilemma.

In our forever shifting, contemporary culture, it is too easy to fall into the "ships passing in the night" syndrome. But our lives don't have to be that way. We can reach out. We can reach up. We can turn our back to the past and "embrace the future." Like Rob Hubbard, we can be proactive in overcoming our loneliness and, with God's help, live a fulfilling and dynamic life. According to John Maxwell, "The difference between greatness and mediocrity is this: When greatness comes to an obstacle, it says there must be a way. If there really is no way, greatness will make a way."

Beware of despairing about yourself:
you are commanded to put your trust in God,
and not in yourself.

—Augustine

# 8

# HOPE FOR A WEEPING WORLD

Weeping may remain for a night,
but rejoicing comes in the morning.
—Ps. 30:5

I (Stan) have fond memories of my first new car—a 1968 Volkswagen Beetle. It had a lot of neat gadgets, including an eight-track tape player hidden in the glove compartment. It also had seat belts, which had recently become a requirement of the law.

One day I asked my friend Kenny Bullock to join me for a ride in my shiny green VW. We drove to see a couple of girls on the west side of town.

We pulled up in front of their house and, like any nervous 17-year-olds, fervently planned our strategy to impress the girls. We mustered the courage to go to the door and ask them out for a ride in my new car.

But we were trapped!

We had both fastened our seat belts, and we couldn't find the release button! Frantically we read the manual, searched the seats, and even asked a passing stranger, all to no avail.

Just about that time the girls came out of the house and noticed us sitting at the curb. With a grin, they came over to the car and asked what we were doing in the neighborhood.

I've often wondered how long they had stood at the front window and watched us sitting there like two idiots, wondering if we were ever going to get out of the car.

We covered our embarrassment by acting as if everything were perfectly fine. We even asked if they wanted a ride in the new car. Their ready acceptance left us scrambling for a reply. Spying the gas gauge, I told them that we'd go get some gas and come right back.

We drove straight to the nearest gas station, where we bought 50 cents worth of gas and asked the attendant to free us from the seat belt trap. Laughing loudly, he reached behind the seats to a well-hidden release button. Finally we were free!

Needless to say, when we went back to pick up the girls, we kept quiet about our seat belt predicament!

My buddy and I could laugh about our confinement in the Volkswagen, for we knew there was a way out—if only we could find it! Many people face painful circumstances in life that leave them feeling trapped and hopeless. The loss, depression, failure, or loneliness they've experienced seems to have shut them off from the rest of the world. They feel that life will never be any different than it is, and their hopelessness and despair have become a prison.

But God wants them to move beyond the despair of their disaster into the bright hope of a victorious relationship with Jesus Christ.

When troubles are deep and your world is dark,
Don't give up hope—TRY GOD.
When life turns sour and you've lost your way,
Don't give up hope—TRY GOD.
When fears stack up and you're sure no one cares,
Don't give up hope—TRY GOD.
When temptation comes knocking and you struggle so,
Don't give up—TRY GOD.

—Author Unknown

## Potholes, Boulders, and Landslides

The journey from weeping to laughter can be a treacherous road, and the traveler may feel as if he or she will never know joy again. The path is often dark, paved with potholes, unexpected boulders, and landslides that might very easily trap the journeyman.

The potholes may be gaping wounds that require healing from God Almighty. They may have been caused by the thoughtless words or the actions of a trusted friend or loved ones. They may have been intentional, or they may have been unintentional. Either way, the hurt makes a lasting impression.

The boulders in that pathway are the issues of unforgiveness. They will block the road and hinder our progress from pain to laughter. They must be removed—and God must do the removing. Our part is to confess their presence to Him. We must ask Him to obliterate all traces of animosity from our hearts.

The landslides are the ploys of Satan as he tries to trap us by causing the cares of life to come crashing down on us. He wrings his hands in glee when the "debris" piles upon us.

But through faith in Christ, he is a defeated foe! As we bring the debris before the Lord, confessing our inadequacy to get rid of it ourselves and our total confidence in His ability to free us, we will see the way gradually clear.

We can claim the promise Joshua made to the leaders of Israel as they faced their enemy, "The LORD your God himself will drive them out of your way. He will push them out before you, and you will take possession of their land, as the LORD your God promised you" (Josh. 23:5).

## Healing

When Christ ministered on the earth, He healed a wide range of physical needs. But He also touched people who had experienced emotional trauma or loss. Nearly 20 percent of the Gospels is devoted to Jesus' healing ministry. Out of 3,779 verses in the four

Gospels, 727 specifically relate to the miracles of Jesus. Twenty-six times in the New Testament He performed miracles—and those are just the miracles that were documented. He is truly the Great Physician!

In John 10:9-10 Jesus said, "I am the gate; whoever enters through me will be saved. He will come in and go out, and find pasture. The thief comes only to steal and kill and destroy; I have come that they may have life, and have it to the full." This fullness of life touches every part of our being—body, mind, and spirit.

A friend told me (Stan) about a highly productive peach tree in his backyard. He picked bushels of luscious peaches and "put them into the ministry" (he's a minister).

He said that one day he noticed a branch with peaches that were rotting. Curious as to the cause, he closely examined the tree. Then he made the discovery: from a distance, the branch looked as if it were a part of the tree, but on closer examination he found that it had split from the trunk and was partially broken off. The fruit had rotted because the source of its nourishment was gone.

The wholeness of the branch came from its being connected to the trunk—the main source. Probably the weight of snow or ice, or the winds of a storm, had been too much to bear. The branch then separated from its only hope for wholeness.

Likewise, wholeness comes from being connected to Christ.

In 1996 George Gallup and Heubert Benson
polled 1,200 people over the age of 18. . . .
30% reported a remarkable healing in their lifetime
related to a physical or psychological problem.
42% attributed the healing to Jesus Christ.
89% experienced a deeper walk with God
as a result of their healing.[1]

You know you are being healed when . . .
You have begun the journey of forgiving
the person who injured you.
You can talk about the issues
that once gave you great pain.
You feel no need to emotionally isolate yourself
from your family and friends.
You have gotten off your "bed"
and are moving forward.
You have stopped basing your identity
upon your past.[2]

—Debra White Smith


It was good for me to be afflicted
so that I might learn your decrees.

—Ps. 119:7


## Restoration

Healing restores a person to his or her previous normal functions. God is able to perform that restoration. Sometimes the healing is instantaneous, but more often it involves a process—especially when concerning emotional wounds and traumatic loss.

Sometimes the Lord uses the skills of medical and psychological professionals to facilitate that healing, such as doctors, nurses, counselors, or hospital technicians. But be assured that any ability they may have was given to them by way of God's knowledge. And know in your heart that all healing ultimately comes from Christ. "He himself bore our sins in his body on the tree, so that we might die to sins and live for righteousness; by his wounds you have been healed" (1 Pet. 2:24).

Do you need emotional, spiritual, or physical healing? Do you have a friend who needs such healing? Follow these simple suggestions:

- **Ask spiritual leaders in your church to lay hands on you and pray for your healing.** "A man with leprosy came to him and begged him on his knees, 'If you are willing, you can make me clean'" (Mark 1:40).
- **Request the use of anointing oil.** "Is any one of you sick? He should call the elders of the church to pray over him and anoint him with oil in the name of the Lord" (James 5:14).
- **Commit to developing intimacy with Jesus Christ by simply being in His presence.** "Be still, and know that I am God" (Ps. 46:10, NKJV).

## The Boulder of Unforgiveness

The second trap that hinders our journey from weeping to laughter is the boulder of unforgiveness. The English word *forgive* literally means "to give away or to give up." C. Neil Strait says, "Where forgiveness is the attitude of life, there happiness and joy are welcome guests. Genuine forgiveness unclogs the heart and lets love flow again. It unshackles life!"[3] Certainly, forgiveness facilitates the healing of the wounds that Satan has made.

But the type of forgiveness we need transcends any human endeavors. In Matt. 18 we read that "Peter came to Jesus and asked, 'Lord, how many times shall I forgive my brother when he sins against me? Up to seven times?' Jesus answered, 'I tell you, not seven times, but seventy-seven times'" (vv. 21-22).

For Peter to suggest even seven times was magnanimous on his part. At that time, most understood that if you suffered with a friend through three challenges to a relationship, you had done what was reasonably expected. But Peter must have thought he had outdone himself. Perhaps his relationship with a friend had suffered seven setbacks. Now Peter wonders,

When is forgiveness perilous?

When is forgiveness outrageous?

Isn't there a reasonable limit?

Jesus' answer of "seventy-seven times" means that our forgiving spirit should encompass all areas of life.

A person with a spirit of genuine forgiveness doesn't wait for a particular condition to forgive. Genuine forgiveness decides before any conflict occurs. This is the kind of forgiveness Jesus exhibited on the Cross. Not only did He make forgiveness available to everyone who had sinned before His death, but He also made forgiveness available for all those who would sin against Him in the years, decades, and centuries to come. True forgiveness cannot be contained. It spills out into every area of life, overflowing into our relationships with security and love.

However, we cannot extend this type of forgiveness unless we first experience it, unless we truly see ourselves as desperately needing forgiveness from the Father.

## The Forgiven Servant

After Jesus told Peter he should forgive 77 times, He related the story of a servant whose gigantic debt was canceled. At that time, the average day's wage was 17 cents, and in comparison, the servant owed the equivalent of all the gold in Fort Knox! After the king canceled the servant's debt, he went to a fellow servant who owed him 17 dollars, strangled him, and had him thrown into prison.

When the king heard about the unforgiving servant, he arranged to have the once-pardoned man tortured in jail until he could pay back all he owed. Of course, the servant's plight was then hopeless. He could never repay what he owed.

The same is true of us.

Until we realize just how much we owe the Lord, and just how unworthy of forgiveness we are . . .

Until we see ourselves at the base of the Cross, blood splattered on our hands, holding the hammer that drove rusty nails through Jesus' flesh . . .

Until we truly understand that without the grace of God, we could be that adulterer, that murderer, that molester, that cheater, that liar, that slanderer . . .

Until we truly come to a gut-wrenching knowledge that we owe the Lord far more than the equivalent of all the gold in Fort Knox—we'll never be able to truly forgive anyone else.

When we were unlovable, God redeemed us and gave us an inheritance in heaven.

Forgiveness is not optional. Further, true forgiveness does not require an apology from the offender. While having someone ask our forgiveness is great, our forgiveness should never hinge on the perpetrator's repentance. True forgiveness comes from God himself, is unconditional, and extends to others, whether or not invited.

True forgiveness releases the offense into the Lord's hands, does not seek revenge or require the offender's penance. You may say, "That's not humanly possible!" You're right! As human beings, we can never produce this type of forgiveness. This gift comes only from God, an imparting of himself to us.

Jesus loved a world that hated Him
He stretched out His hands to them,
And they pierced those healing hands with spikes.
He walked down the dusty roads of Jerusalem,
Bringing good news,
And they nailed those precious feet to a tree.
He blessed them, and they cursed Him.
They mocked Him, and He prayed,
"Father, forgive them."
Who am I not to pray the same?
The servant is not above his or her Lord.

—Stan Toler

## Layers of Forgiveness

None of this is to say forgiveness is easy or that we will never struggle with issues of forgiveness. Furthermore, forgiveness for deep injuries can at times come in "layers."

Consider the layers in an onion. Those layers can be peeled away one at a time until there is nothing left. Likewise, God desires to peel away the layers of our unforgiveness until there is nothing left. Evangelist Nathan Covington says, "There's healing in the peeling." And if we will let Him, God will peel away the animosity until nothing but peace remains.

The good news is that even in the face of our human struggles, we can throw ourselves upon the mercy of God. By His mercy and grace, He will lead us down that heartwarming path from tears to laughter.

## Beginning the Journey

Are you unsure where you should begin your journey to forgiveness? Here are three important steps in finding forgiveness:

- **Repent.** Ask God to forgive you. Ask Him to cover the resentments with His cleansing blood. "If we walk in the light, as he is in the light, we have fellowship with one another, and the blood of Jesus, his Son, purifies us from all sin. If we claim to be without sin, we deceive ourselves and the truth is not in us. If we confess our sins, he is faithful and just and will forgive us our sins and purify us from all unrighteousness" (1 John 1:7-9).

- **Make a choice.** As an act of the will, forgive those who have offended you, whether or not you feel like it. When unforgiving thoughts barge in upon your thoughts, ask the Lord to impart the self-discipline to control your thoughts. "Bear with each other and forgive whatever grievances you may have against one another. Forgive as the Lord forgave you" (Col. 3:13).

- **Rely on God's grace.** "It is by grace you have been saved, through faith—and this not from yourselves, it is the gift of God—not by works, so that no one can boast" (Eph. 2:8-9).

- **Ask God to show you** the one you are struggling to forgive as He sees the person. For me (Debra) this opened the flood-gates of pity upon the person who molested me and freed me of any and all bitterness.
- **Pray that God** will remove that person or the effects of that situation from your mind, spirit, and soul. This prayer, though simple, began my (Debra's) deliverance from 20 years of struggling with the torment of sexual abuse.

## Seeking God

Satan doesn't want us to make that journey from tears to laughter. He doesn't want us to put our hope in God for healing. He doesn't want us to live victorious lives. He would rather we be trapped in the potholes of our wounds, forever halted by the boulders of unforgiveness, landslides of trouble heaped upon us. But Satan doesn't have to have the last word. We have a choice either to empower him, keeping ourselves trapped, or to break free and move forward to a bright, hopeful future, impacting others for the Lord.

The vehicle that will speed us forward in victorious living is an intimate, lasting encounter with the Creator of the universe. As Christians, we have a power available to us that will stop Satan in his tracks: a power for healing after losses, a power for forgiveness, a power for learning to laugh again.

That will happen as we take the time to daily encounter God. A hit-and-miss friendship with the Lord only opens us up to Satan's attacks. Spiritual weakness allows him to pour the acid of self-righteousness, hatred, and unforgiveness into the very wounds he has afflicted us with.

According to evangelist and missionary leader Tom Hermiz, "Bitterness remembers the details!" And Satan wants to fill our souls with enough bitterness to forever emblazon on our minds the details of the wrongs committed against us. But when he sees us on our knees, he knows his defeat is near!

The moment you start to resent people, you become
their slave. They control your dreams, absorb your
digestion, rob you of your peace of mind and good will,
and take away the pleasure of your work. They ruin
your religion and nullify your prayers. You cannot
take a vacation without their going along.
They destroy your freedom of mind and hound you
wherever you go. There is no way to escape people you
resent. They are with you when you are awake; they
invade your privacy when you sleep. They are close
beside you when you eat, when you drive your car,
and when you are on the job.
You can never have efficiency or happiness. They
influence even the tone of your voice. They require you
to take medicine for indigestion, headaches, and loss
of energy. They even steal your last moment of
consciousness before you go to sleep.
So if you want to be a slave, harbor resentment.

—Author Unknown

## Wrapped in Joy

Our healing, hope, and joy are in direct proportion to the time we spend in communion with the Lord—not asking for a thing, but rather soaking up His presence and allowing His spirit to wrap our soul in joy.

Looking back on the loss of my father, I (Stan) can see that, even as a child, I used the quietness of my bedroom to commune with God. I believe those times with my Heavenly Father empowered me to live a life of victory.

I (Debra) can likewise testify to God's healing power. This issue of soaking in God's presence proves that He is truly our calm in the storm. I'm truly in awe of the miracles that God has performed in my spirit, mind, and emotions.

Certainly God often uses a Christian psychiatrist or counselor to further His healing purposes. For example, I have greatly benefited from the counsel of Christian psychologists such as those heard on well-known Christian radio programs. And I have been enriched by a host of insightful authors such as James Dobson, David Seamands, and Gary Smalley. However, no earthly psychologist can bring about the miracle of filling our souls with singing when we have been doused with sorrow. Only the Lord performs such a miracle.

The bottom line is that Satan does not want us to commune with the Father about our hurts. When we accept the invitation of the Scriptures—"Come, let us bow down in worship, let us kneel before the LORD our Maker; for he is our God and we are the people of his pasture" (Ps. 95:6-7)—Satan knows that he has lost the battle. Therefore, he will throw every excuse imaginable in our paths to stop this communion. The closer we're drawn to the Lord, the more Satan will increase his attacks in these areas of our spiritual lives:

- **Obeying the Word of God.** For instance, an unforgiving spirit will hinder our communication with the Lord, stunt our spiritual growth, and trap us in the past. But the Bible says, "Blessed are they who keep his statutes and seek him with all their heart" (Ps. 119:2).

- **Putting our hope in the Word.** "I rise before dawn and cry for help; I have put my hope in your word" (Ps. 119:147). Even when we might feel void of any positive emotions, we can stake our hopes on God's faithfulness and the promises found in the Bible.

- **Claiming God's promises.** "My comfort in my suffering is this: Your promise preserves my life" (Ps. 119:50). If God has promised, we can believe Him! No matter what our circumstances, God is still there, still ready to bind our wounds and bring healing to our souls.

- **Submitting to God.** When we hold back any part of our will from the Lord, we automatically give Satan an opportunity to keep us forever trapped in sorrow. James wrote, "Submit yourselves, then, to God" (James 4:7).
- **Rebuking Satan.** "Resist the devil, and he will flee from you. Come near to God and he will come near to you" (James 4:7-8). I (Debra) am personally exercising this in the area of forgiveness.

Even after forgiving those who have harmed me in great ways, Satan would often entrap me to harbor resentment for small misunderstandings. I'm learning to immediately rebuke Satan in his attempts to taint my soul with animosity. Notice that in this verse the action of coming near to God immediately follows the act of rebuking Satan. As long as we allow Satan time to control our thoughts, our coming near to God will be hindered. Remember that Satan wants to see Christians defeated, hopeless, and crying—not victorious, trusting, and joyful. However, we do not have to battle him alone, "For the battle is not yours, but God's" (2 Chron. 20:15).

"I will turn their mourning into gladness; I will give them comfort and joy instead of sorrow. . . . Restrain your voice from weeping and your eyes from tears, for your work will be rewarded," declares the LORD. "They will return from the land of the enemy. So there is hope for your future," declares the LORD. "Your children will return to their own land."

—Jer. 31:13, 16-17

## From Mourning to Gladness

The journey from mourning to gladness may be difficult, but many have successfully completed it. My (Debra's) father, Gaylon L. White, is a living example. His testimony will inspire anyone who is seeking to move from despair to joy:

When I said yes to God's call to preach, it was like being saved all over again. I didn't touch the ground for two weeks, because I was walking on air. I had struggled trying to decide if my mother was calling me, if this was my idea, or if God was really calling. It was God!

But after only five-and-one-half short years in the ministry, I was out. My first assignment had been difficult, but God had seen me through. And after only five months in my second assignment, I resigned due to family issues. I wondered how life had gotten so bad in one short year and how life could be so cruel as to destroy my hopes and dreams.

Soon, I found a job at a meat packing plant. After two years of struggling, my marriage ended, and we divorced. I was miserable. God had given me a call to preach, and I could no longer fulfill that call. I remember driving down the highway, praying that God would open a door for me to preach once more. The desire to be back in the pulpit was almost overwhelming. One day I told a fellow pastor, "Don't take your ministry for granted. It could be gone tomorrow." I knew that no one wanted a divorced, single father of two teenagers to pastor a church. Besides, I hadn't finished my pastoral studies, so I wasn't even ordained.

Finally God at last gave me peace about not being able to fulfill my call to preach. Even though my local church supported me, and I taught Sunday School and served as the Sunday School superintendent, I had to accept that I would never again pastor a church.

Then, after seven years of working as a truck driver, I found a strange thing beginning to happen. I felt as if God was again pointing me toward the preaching ministry. But that seemed odd. After all, I was divorced and single—not a favorable combination. But the pattern of my first call was repeating itself: my job was losing meaning, and people were spontaneously telling me I didn't look like a truck driver or that I needed to be pastoring a church.

After a lot of prayer, I felt led to consult with a retired minister about the possibilities of my reentering the ministry. I was especially concerned about the divorce issue, but my friend encouraged me. So I contacted a denominational leader, who also encouraged me. Bit by bit, I watched as the Lord miraculously began piecing my ministry back together. I asked for a local preacher's license, which my church granted. Then I asked the denomination to reinstate me in the pastoral course of study. At that time, a person was allowed 8 years to finish. Although it had been 12 years since I first started, I asked to be declared "an exception, due to unusual circumstances." They gave me a second chance.

I memorized study guides while driving down interstate highways. I stayed home on weekends, except for church, and did my reading assignments. With God's help, I finished almost two years of study in one year and graduated. You don't blow a second chance!

At this point I decided I would have to be an evangelist, since I didn't feel that any church would be interested in calling an unmarried man as pastor. I was satisfied with remaining single. However, a friend told me I ought to get acquainted with Mamie Martin, a lady I had known years before who was now a widow. I hadn't seen Mamie for years and didn't believe that we would hit it off, so I told my friend I wasn't interested.

But God had other plans. A friend invited me to revival services at his church. The night I attended, he acknowledged the visitors who were present, one of whom was Mamie. When the service was over, I turned to leave. There she stood, wearing a white blouse with a big red bow. I'll never forget that red bow. The years had made Mamie even more attractive. I looked at the woman in whom I had said I wasn't interested and decided we needed to get together and talk over old times!

I was scheduled to preach a revival in another town, and I asked Mamie to have dinner with me before I left. Soon we became "an item," and we dated for nine months.

We eventually realized we were in a serious relationship and needed to make a decision about marriage. She had to decide if God was calling her to be a preacher's wife. Soon she made her decision and was waiting for me to decide. As I returned home from visiting her one night, I prayed that God would give me clear guidance. I lay down for the night, opened my Bible, and the Lord led me to Prov. 18:22—"He who finds a wife finds a good thing, and obtains favor from the LORD" (NKJV). I couldn't believe it! There's no context to give the verse alternate meaning, and I strongly believe in interpreting verses according to their context. Neither do I believe in randomly picking scripture as a promise. This had never happened to me before and hasn't happened since. But I wasn't satisfied. I asked God to give me a clear inner witness to go with the scripture that marriage to Mamie was God's will for me. On the next visit, instead of the uncertainty, God gave me the clear witness I had asked for.

Later, on August 18, 1988, in Dallas, Texas, with my new wife, Mamie, at my side, and the approval of all six general superintendents, I was ordained an elder in the Church of the Nazarene. I said "evangelist" when I had no wife. God said "pastor" and gave me Mamie.

Life can be awful and can dump on you, leaving you a hopeless bundle of despair. I don't understand all that happened in my life. I never will. But God does. I think of the words of Joseph to his brothers when they feared for their lives at the death of their father: "Don't be afraid. Am I in the place of God? You intended to harm me, but God intended it for good to accomplish what is now being done" (Gen. 50:19-20). We have a wonderful God who can turn the worst into the best. I have been on a journey that began in mourning. Thank God, it has ended in joy!

> Weeping may remain for a night,
> but rejoicing comes in the morning.
>
> —Ps. 30:5

## Hope in the Darkness

You may be discouraged about the prospect of finding joy in your life. At times it may seem to you that there is no hope of escaping the difficult circumstances of your life. But remember that if you choose to fix your eyes on Jesus, cling to Him, and rely on His strength, He will see you through. God is greater than your heartache.

Here are some things that heartache cannot do:

- **Heartache cannot cripple love.** "How great is the love the Father has lavished on us, that we should be called the children of God! And that is what we are! The reason the world does not know us is that it did not know him. Dear friends, now we are children of God, and what we will be has not yet been made known. But we know that when he appears, we shall be like him, for we shall see him as he is. Everyone who has this hope in him purifies himself, just as he is pure" (1 John 3:1-3).

- **Heartache cannot smother faith.** "Since we are surrounded by such a great cloud of witnesses, let us throw off everything that hinders and the sin that so easily entangles, and let us run with perseverance the race marked out for us. Let us fix our eyes on Jesus, the author and perfecter of our faith, who for the joy set before him endured the cross, scorning its shame, and sat down at the right hand of the throne of God" (Heb. 12:1-2).

- **Heartache cannot eradicate courage.** "Though we live in the world, we do not wage war as the world does. The weapons we fight with are not the weapons of the world. On the contrary, they have divine power to demolish strongholds" (2 Cor. 10:3-4).

- **Heartache cannot annihilate good memories.** "The memory of the righteous will be a blessing" (Prov. 10:7).
- **Heartache cannot shatter compassion.** "As the father has compassion on his children, so the LORD has compassion on those who fear him; for he knows how we are formed, he remembers that we are dust" (Ps. 103:13-14).
- **Heartache cannot destroy hope.** "Now we know that if the earthly tent we live in is destroyed, we have a building from God, an eternal house in heaven, not built by human hands" (2 Cor. 5:1).
- **Heartache has no power over praise.** "O LORD, you are my God; I will exalt you and praise your name, for in perfect faithfulness you have done marvelous things, things planned long ago" (Isa. 25:1).
- **Heartache cannot erase the fact of the Resurrection.** "I am the resurrection and the life. He who believes in me will live, even though he dies" (John 11:25).

Don't allow heartache to keep you its prisoner. You can begin the journey to gladness today. Here are important action steps to healing and wholeness:

- **Acknowledge Jesus as Lord of your life.** "Submit yourselves, then, to God. Resist the devil, and he will flee from you" (James 4:7).
- **Boldly ask in faith for God's healing touch.** "If you believe, you will receive whatever you ask for in prayer" (Matt. 21:22).
- **Be specific about your need.** "Praise the LORD, O my soul, and forget not all his benefits—who forgives all your sins and heals all your diseases" (Ps. 103:2-3).
- **Witness to others concerning your healing miracle.** "As Peter traveled about the country, he went to visit the saints in Lydda. There he found a man named Aeneas, a paralytic who had

been bedridden for eight years. 'Aeneas,' Peter said to him, 'Jesus Christ heals you. Get up and take care of your mat.' Immediately Aeneas got up. All those who lived in Lydda and Sharon saw him and turned to the Lord" (Acts 9:32-35).

Lord, make me an instrument of Thy peace:
Where there is hatred, let me sow love;
Where there is injury, pardon;
Where there is doubt, faith;
Where there is despair, hope;
Where there is darkness, light;
Where there is sadness, joy;
O Divine Master, grant that I may not so much seek
To be consoled as console,
To be understood as to understand,
To be loved as to love;
For it is in giving that we receive;
It is in pardoning that we are pardoned;
It is in dying that we are born to eternal life!

—Francis of Assisi

## The Path to Healing

While writing the last pages of this book, I (Debra) visited my dear friend Frances Shaw. I read my version of the "Beeps Anonymous" story to her to make certain I had stated everything accurately. We shared rolls of laughter, just as we did the night we found the source of the beep. Then, as we discussed her health, Frances and I cried together. Suffering from both kidney failure and a painful form of cancer, she's facing death.

At times I find it hard to believe that this beautiful, vivacious woman who has been my "cheerleader" is no longer going to fill my life with her bright spirit and encouragement. Even as I write this, I'm crying, because her death will leave a painful, gaping hole in my life.

Before we ended our visit, Frances and I wrapped our arms around each other and prayed together. We wept. We laughed. And she tearfully told me, "I'll never forget you. I love you like my own daughter."

I expressed my own love for her and thanked her for the painting she was giving me, one she created herself. The work of art depicts a path leading to a gate, from the gate to the mountains, and from the mountains to a sunrise. Frances said, "This is a symbol of always looking to the future." I hung the painting in my dining room. And as I gaze upon it, I remember the woman who has been a friend and mother to me. More than that, I remember to always, always, take the path that leads to the Light, to healing, to a future bright with hope.

We (Stan and Debra) have found that Light. And our prayer is that you have seen enough of the brilliance that you will step into the arms of Christ and find your healing—a healing that will turn your hurts to unexplainable joy.

On this earth, we have merely a note;
the melody is beyond.

—Fulton J. Sheen

# NOTES

## Chapter 1

1. Bruce Larson, *What God Wants to Know* (San Francisco: Harper, 1993), 59-60. Copyright © 1993 by Bruce Larson. Reprinted by permission of HarperCollins Publishers, Inc.

2. Adapted from *An Encyclopedia of Humor,* comp. Lowell D. Streiker (Nashville: Hendrickson Publishers, 1998), 121.

3. Jefferson Graham and Arlene Vigoda, "Robert Young Knew Life's Best," *USA Today,* July 23, 1998, D-1.

4. Patrick Morley, *Walking with Christ in the Details of Life* (Nashville: Thomas Nelson Publishers, 1992), 245.

## Chapter 2

1. *Webster's Dictionary,* 1828, s.v. "depression."

2. *Webster's New Collegiate Dictionary* (Springfield, Mass.: G. & C. Merriam Co., 1975), s.v. "depression."

3. *Pastoral Psychology,* July 1998, 431.

4. National Institute of Health, brochure from the Oklahoma Department of Healath, n.d.

5. Charles R. Swindoll, *Maybe It's Time to Laugh Again: Experiencing Outrageous Joy* (Anaheim, Calif.: Insight for Living, 1992), 102-3.

6. Adapted from *Encyclopedia of 7700 Illustrations,* comp. Paul Lee Tan (Rockville, Md.: Assurance Publishers, 1984), 1507.

## Chapter 3

1. Adapted from Stan Toler, *God Has Never Failed Me, but He's Sure Scared Me to Death a Few Times* (Tulsa, Okla.: Honor Books, 2000), 67-69. Used by permission.

2. Adapted from ibid., 155. Used by permission.

## Chapter 4

1. George Henson, "Faith Grows in Shooting's Shadow," *Baptist Standard,* October 13, 1999, 1, 10. Used by permission.

## Chapter 5

1. Stephen J. Lennox, "The Powers of Chaos," *Illustrated Bible Life,* September-October-November 1999, 25-26.

2. Ibid., 26.

3. Robert Q. Bailey, "Following Jesus' Itinerary," *Illustrated Bible Life,* September-October-November 1999, 8.

4. From sermon by Terry Toler. Copyright 2000 by Terry Toler. Used by permission.

## Chapter 6

1. C. S. Lewis, *A Grief Observed* (San Francisco: Harper, 1994), 67.

2. Kenneth W. Osbeck, *101 Hymn Stories* (Grand Rapids: Kregel Publishers, 1982), 58-59.

3. James Clay and Frank Clay, *The Grief Recovery Book* (New York: Harper and Row, 1981), 67-69.

4. Norman Vincent Peale, *This Incredible Century* (Wheaton, Ill.: Tyndale House Publishers, 1991), 188.

## Chapter 7

1. James C. Hefley, *Life Changes* (Wheaton, Ill.: Tyndale House Publishers, 1984), 149.

2. Lee Strobel, *Vital Ministry Magazine,* April 1998, 33.

3. Lloyd John Ogilvie, *The Bush Is Still Burning* (Waco, Tex.: Word Books, 1980), 160.

4. *People,* December 2, 1996, 72.

5. Steve Brown, "Forgiven and Forgotten," *Key Life* 14:2 (April—June 1999), 1.

6. Personal interview with Jerry Brecheisen. Used by permission.

7. Ogilvie, *Bush Is Still Burning,* 162.

8. Adapted from Toler, *God Has Never Failed Me,* 99. Used by permission.

## Chapter 8

1. George H. Gallup and Heubert Benson, *Emerging Trends* 19:6 (June 1997), 4.

2. Debra White Smith, *More than Rubies: Becoming a Woman of Godly Influence* (Kansas City: Beacon Hill Press of Kansas City, 2000), 135.

3. C. Neil Strait, chapel service, Olivet Nazarene University, October 1978.